Real Estate Investing with No Money Down

How to Retire Early, Create a Lifetime of Cash Flow, and Discover the Secret Strategies to Consistently Generating Over $10,000 per Month in Passive Income

By

Bob Lee

Table of Contents

INTRODUCTION

There are several ways to get into real estate investment. Before picking up this book to read, you have inevitably had some exposure or at the very least, an idea of what it is that real estate means.

Now, owning property is not always easy, but there are several advantages to it if you can break into the market. Real estate is one of the oldest and most well-known classes of investment, and there are different ways to go about it. This book will act as a guide in opening your eyes to the vast array of opportunities that abound and how to make the best use of them.

One of the best financial decisions to make is investing in real estate; however, many people have the same problem when they want to invest in real estate: they have no money to spend, and their credit is too poor to get the loans. The good news is that you can invest in real estate even without pay, and these are the strategies that will be explored in this book.

But first, a few hard truths:

Not everyone can buy real estate without money. It is possible, but it is hard and will require a lot of work and commitment from you to make it work. It will also need you to be ready to make some losses and to learn from your mistakes.

You may want to end up like one of those people who talk a lot about real estate but never quite get it done. Do not be that person.

If you ever feel stuck even before you have started, the strategies in this book will help you out. But, if you still feel stuck afterward, then maybe it is high time you check out other investment opportunities.

Generally, real estate investment is a great investment option because it can help you generate a passive income that can last until the end of time. And it will get even better with the right investment strategies as you are about to find out in this book. You will learn how to invest in real estate and how you can enjoy excellent returns on investment; incredible taxes and how you can begin to build wealth that will last.

First, we will cover the basics.

WHY REAL ESTATE IS A GOOD INVESTMENT?

Real estate is dealing in property consisting of lands and buildings. It can also be said to include rights above the ground and underground rights and rights on the earth. It is the property that consists of land and buildings as well as natural resources, uncultivated and cultivated flora and fauna, crops, and animals, water and aquatic life and minerals components of the earth. How investors can make money through real estate are, to be landlords of rental properties, real estate trading, I.e., flipping, real estate investment groups, and real estate investment trusts (REITs). For one to venture in Real estate investment one need to have background knowledge of what constitutes real estate to start with, real estate comes in various categories, they are:

RESIDENTIAL REAL ESTATE

These are physical properties built for living. It can be a new building, and it can as well be a resale house. Residential real estate includes single-family homes, multifamily homes, townhouse, duplexes, vacation homes, rental properties, to mention a few. Residential real estate is mainly for the occupant who wants to reside singly or with their family in the comfort of their homes. Many factors are attributes

7

to a customer determining the choice of residence, they are, location of the property, the income of the family, the size of the family, etc.

COMMERCIAL REAL ESTATE

Commercial real estate is used for income-generating purposes. Building for commercial purposes is shopping centers, hotels, offices, educational centers, apartment buildings, health care facilities, rental buildings for rent or lease. A commercial building can be free-standing or shopping malls. The factor that determines retail real estate sale is the location of the property, the type of commodity sold or service rendered, the financial capacity of the buyer, etc.

INDUSTRIAL REAL ESTATE

Industrial real estate is usually for manufacturing, distributing or to put in a warehouse what is produced. Industrial real estate can be used for research, storage and also be used for distribution of goods. Industrial properties include park, mines, farmstead, and are usually occupying a vast area.

LAND

The Land is the solid layer of Earth that is not fully covered by water. Most of the human activity has occurred in inland areas that support agriculture, habitat, and various natural resources. The land is a real estate property, and it includes vacation land, tourist centers, zoos, farms, cattle ranch. It can also be an area developed too early or not at all.

IMPORTANCE OF REAL ESTATE

Real estate is a modest and reasonable form of getting income. Most real estates appreciate over time. Hence it offers a substantial financial advantage and independence for people who invest in it.

Real estate is useful for building equity for the future. Investment is the asset that constitutes one's net worth. As one build equity, one has the leverage to acquire additional rental properties and increase cash flow.

One can invest directly in real estate by buying properties or indirectly by obtaining shares in Real Estate Investment Trust (REITS) or securities on mortgage

Real estate is a real and tangible property made up of land and everything on it, over it, and under it giving the owner of the property multiple advantages.

Another important thing about real estate is that it is without limitations; it can be suitable for individuals as well as commercial. Real estate is also of great import because it is valuable and brings stable for a form of investment for every investing actor be it individual or commercial

Real estate provides a steady source of income. If chosen wisely by getting an excellent location ,a person may be assured of a constant income for a relatively long period. One can save for the future or even plan for early retirement and not having to wait for the traditional retirement or pension. With real estate, one can generate a passive income, which is valid and a consistent way of getting money. It is a stable means of getting money for a very long time.

Since real property is appreciated over time, it gives investors a long term financial security.

Real property is not subjected to individual proprietary tax. There is also tax relief for property depreciation, maintenance cost, insurance, legal fee.

Nobody loves to take orders from anyone. And everyone wants to be a boss! And this is guaranteed in real estate. Autonomy is also one advantage of real estate investment. Owners of the property enjoy ownerships, as they are their "own boss" and they will eventually decide how much to charge and who will manage the property itself.   Hence a person has total control over the property,   tenants, and resources. Instead of waiting for employment opportunities, he/she will be able to create employment for him/herself and others, such as contractors.

Inflation is when much money is chasing few goods. Owners of real properties do not see the rise as a threat to their business and because the cost of living increases so also does the price of real property. This eventually will pump cash flow to the real estate investor, and as the economy grows, the demand for real estate increases rents higher, thus creating higher value on properties.

WHY SHOULD YOU CREATE MULTIPLE SOURCE OF INCOME

A Various sources of income is when one earns money from different sources. It is one of the keys to financial independence and early retirement. Is a form of passive income where one works and generates a stream of income with little or no effort afterward. It is a form of side work, apart from the main work one does. Passive income is income earned with small activities through different ventures, which require little effort. It is a multiple source of income that is derived from rental property, limited partnership, or other business that one is not fully involved with. It is sometimes taxable. It is a way of making money while one sleeps. It is a point where one's asset is working for someone, but the first one has to invest time, money, energy. Creating more than one income can be lots of work, especially when one already has one source of employment and want to create more. There are several benefits on having several sources of income, and it makes it worth the effort.

FORMS OF MULTIPLE SOURCE OF INCOME

Instances of multiple sources of income a person can engage in are:

- One can invest in a high yielding savings account that has a top percent interest. All you need is to exceed the fixed deposit and see yourself earning at leisure.
- One can also invest in high dividend stock which gives income at a yearly value
- One can also invest in real estate with REIT. With REIT, a person does not have to worry about the management of the property; the company manages on one's behalf.
- One can also invest in a corporate bond. Corporate bonds are issued by corporations and are used by companies to fund their business.
- One can also start an already neglected blog or buy a new one. It is highly profitable yet extremely cheap. One can use it and created a lot of value for people as well
- One can also start an online course or guide. One can add video lesson, a checklist for completing steps one recommend for video lessons, interviews with same mind expert, etc

- One can also write an eBook. One can sell it on one's website or offer for an affiliate arrangement with others. On can also sell the book and get royalties.
- One can also be taking up the paid survey for companies from the corner of one's room and get paid
- One can be a freelance writer.
- One can work as a virtual assistant,
- One can also offer a service or selling a product, or creating a product and also place an online ad
- One can start a passionate project like going into music, makeup, etc

GETTING STARTED

The benefits of multiple sources of income are diverse, and it outweighs the difficulty. If you build additional income related to your existing home business, to add more income streams to your business, you need to

*Plan the business. Write Your Main Business Product or Services

Create Spokes from your main business and Create Spoke from These Categories with Ideas on How You Can Make Money from Them

*Give attention to Passive Income Streams That You Create One at a time until They Continue to Generate Income

 Face the Income Streams That Can enlarge Your Business

*Decide on one Income Stream at a Time

Preparing a new stream is the most time-consuming. Avoid jumping into several ideas at one time; don't focus on many areas at once it will exert your efforts and slow you down.

*Wait Until One Income Stream is successful before running to start the Next

If one has several additional income ideas, one has to wait for one to be up and running before starting the next one. One has to work to have the necessary tools in place to help one manage existing income streams.

*Please drop an Income Stream If It Isn't Working

No need for being choked with irrelevance. You want to give your additional income streams the time and effort needed to get them running, but if they don't start generating income or if you loathe it then stop it.

Although adding income streams takes time, creating them within one current business is faster and easier than starting completely new income streams from the beginning. This method of generating additional sources of income works well for any business.

HOW TO CREATE MULTIPLE STREAM OF INCOME USING REAL ESTATE

MINERAL RIGHT DEPOSIT

Mineral Resource is the concentration or occurrence of material of economic value in or on the earth's crust in such form that there are reasonable prospects for eventual commercial extraction. Mineral Resources are further sub-divided, in order of increasing geological confidence, into inferred, Indicated and measured, the property you have has mineral resource; this is a massive way of making money as a real estate investor. Companies in need of these resources can lease the property at a substantial rental price, thereby fetching one a very high income. Such mineral includes crude oil, natural resources like gold, etc., company in need of such product will pay for its exploration.

CONSULTATION FEE

Consultancy fee paid for consulting the service of a real estate investor.

As a real estate investor, when people want to buy or sell the property, you get paid your consultation fee. Also, you might consider professional advice and general consultation. One can also charge for all these consultations.

NOTE

It is an excellent way of getting an additional stream of income in real estate. If one sells a property at a higher price and one is willing to finance part of the sale. One takes a note secured by a property one has ones first stream. If one adds interest to the income and one gets a fair return on the money owed. Each note adds its source of income.

ENGAGE IN RENTALS

On can either choose to rent properties outright to families, students, singles, or you can offer a lease or rent-to-own homeownership opportunity for those who have struggled in the past but still have the dream of homeownership.

Other options for having multiple streams of income through real estate is to have a few rental properties, flips, commercial properties, and a pre-construction deal or vacation condo or Airing rental.

OPTION

One can also increase income by selling the option to purchase one's property that includes rent or lease.

An alternative is nonrefundable. Each option comes with streams of income.

TAX CERTIFICATES

As a real estate investor, there is a plethora of tax advantage connected with real estate. One can also have the government give addition or multiples steam of income by buying tax certificate. One can get many returns from such an investment.

RENT INCREASE

The market value of a property is the rent paid on it. Another way to earn money in real estate investment is through the increase of tenancy rent. May provide an additional source of income to real estate investors.

MAINTENANCE FEE

Maintenance fee is charged over a property to pay down payment as against if the tenant misuse the property. Maintenance fee collection along with other costs such as rents, agent fee, consultancy fee, etc.

Property owners collect maintenance fee from tenant against exegesis of misuse of property. Hence in real estate, the maintenance fee can serve as a source of income if tenant misuse the property. The property owner will not have to use his money to repair the property. Surely another way of earning income

VACANT LAND REVIVING

Many lands lie fallow and aren't placed to use. A real estate investor might decide to use this land to create multiple sources of income.

A bare land that is not in active use can be used to create another source of income. All that the property owner has to do is to be creative about it. He can put the land into use for park, storage building, etc

ONE CAN ALSO TAKE LOAN AGAINST EqUITY

One can also borrow loan against the existing property; it has lower interest rates than other investments. They also typically come with a fixed interest rate is an easy way to get a large sum of money in a short time. In other words, it is a secured loan that is secured by one's home value.

LATE FEE

Late fee is the amount charged over the actual rent if a property if the tenant of property delays in paying. An investor must always charge for late fee payment if the tenant fails to pay up as at when due. That is another way of creating income through most property owners forego due to oversight. As an investor one must be able to separate business from kindness

MERITS OF MULTIPLE SOURCE OF INCOME

SATISFACTION

If one is interested in earning extra cash apart from the main work and does not want to wait until the end of the month as a salary earner, multiple sources of income are the escape route. Various sources of income create an avenue for an individual to earn extra money steadily.

INDEPENDENCE

Another reason to consider multiple sources of income is the independence that is guaranteed. It gives an individual greater satisfaction as one is autonomous and is not receiving orders from anyone.

DIVERSITY

Another essential reason to opt for multiple sources of income is that one must not tie to one income avenue. On is opened to various options. So in the absence of one yielding income at a particular time, the others are generating steady income, and one is not financially stranded.

JOB SECURITY

For employment stability and the need to continually stay in work and generate viable income, multiple sources of income are the solution. With various sources of income, a secured job. Cash flow is intact because one has more than one source of income. With the improvement in technology, these days, ' companies are shutting down because they are losing relevance. Hence technology has made for a secured source of living from one's home

EASE

Another benefit of multiple sources of income is that It's easier to create several small income-producing streams than one large one.

RELIABLE MEANS OF CASH FLOW

It limits the risk of being left without any income. If you are laid off, one has other sources to help you get by. Some income-earning enterprise has seasoned, so when one is not working out, the other is working out.

IT IS ENTERPRISING

To get out of boredom, choose multiple sources of income. It prevents boredom in work by having different things to do every time. You are always doing engaged in gainful activities. One does not relapse to depression.

IT IS SELF FULFILLING

You can create income streams based on your interests, talents, and passions. When you do what you love doing, you experience ease and fulfillment.

THE MYTH IN REAL ESTATE

One should be well-grounded in what one wants to venture into before doing it. Many people are misguided about investing in real estate. The following are fiction people accustomed to before going into real estate.

FLIPPING PROPERTIES IN REAL ESTATE A SURE DOOR TO FINANCIAL INDEPENDENCE...

Says who??? Flipping is merely buying and selling real estate several times within a short period. One needs to know that in flipping more transaction cost are associated also getting a buyer and negotiating deals is strenuous and time-consuming. Hence flipping might not be advisable. Many resources are time-consuming one must be guided to avoid waste of time and resources.

BUYING PROPERTIES, IN THE LONG RUN, PAYS THAN RENTING PROPERTY.

One must look before one leap goes the saying. Feeling it is more advisable to buy real property rather than renting is not always true. The cost of owning a home is far more massive compared to renting a property. Such expenses include property taxes, insurance, utility, home maintenance fees, significant repairs, plus the overall expensive purchase price.

LEVERAGE AND TAX REDUCTION IS SAVOURY

All that glitters is not gold! As regards advantage and tax reduction, there is still much tendency to lose money. Leverage assure investors that the price of the house will increase, but it is not always so in every case. Real estate depreciates sometimes. So it is two sides of a coin. One must prepare to lose before putting out one's hard-earned money.

For tax, the amount one pays in an owing house is higher than rentals. Though one saves money on mortgage interest through tax breaks.

Both factors conclusively are not enough reason for investing in real estate.

LAND APPRECIATE

Land appreciates, but it depreciates too! Shocking? The property enjoys sometimes but in some cases considering some factors depreciates also. Because of constant emergence in developing countries for the past decades, capital is seen to be appreciated, but in developed countries where demand for property is not with menace, because of technological advancement or multiple streams of income, the need for a property as an essential factor of production has diminished .

YOU NEED ONE VERY HUGE CAPITAL TO STARTUP

Although investing in real property requires much, but one does not have to be so costly to start. There are lots to the alternative to having a considerable capital, which includes one can partner with reliable persons, and one can take loam, one can flip a property.

HUGE RENT SCARE OFF TENANT

 Most investors are scared to add to the rental charges even when the amount charged is below the rental value. Advised investors make sure that one must rent at a low rate to keep the tenants. Even at the expense of one's profit and the present market value. As an investor, when contemplating increasing the rent, one can start by growing gradually year in a year till it reaches the actual market value. Having done that, one does not risk losing one's tenant.

ONE MUST CUT COST TO GET GOOD PROFIT

Apart from the cost of a property, one should consider other factors for the making of an excellent rental. If one buys property in a low-cost area, the rent charge will also be low. So it is advisable to find suitable properties that can yield high cash flow. The cheap property comes with lots of capital to fix, and if the quality is not right, the chances are that one won't be able to charge a lot of rent. Cutting cost by buying a cheap property or using affordable product isn't always better for generating a reasonable income. In the long run, one is not doing oneself any favor. When purchasing a property, one should not only consider the cost but also other factors like location, accessibility, etc.

SCARCITY OF LAND

For where? Some estate agents promote the belief that land is scarce; hence if one has the opportunity, it should be seen as a golden opportunity and should grab it , thinking maybe that the human population explosion will soon override the land available. This is actually false; technological development has made it possible for more efficient use of the property. Also, studies conducted state that the population of the world will eventually stabilize as population growth has reached its peak; therefore, the number of people will remain the way it is or less.

THE RIGHT MINDSET TO INVEST IN REAL ESTATE

Being successful in real estate requires one to have a good vibe and shape ones thought towards positivity that will guarantee success. Success does not grow on a platter of gold, and for one to be successful in real estate, one has to be consistent and proactive. The following are some steps to consider to become successful in real estate.

STRUCTURE YOUR BUSINESS AND STRATEGIZE WELL

Since the goal of every Real estate investment us to increase wealth, one needs to make sure one's business is well structured and legally sanctioned, this boils down to how one handles legal and tax matters.

When strategizing, you have to decide which aspect of real estate you want to engage in whether it is flip or short sales or note sales. And also have to ask oneself the kind of life one wants and think of what one wishes the future to look. One must rake actions that fit into one's vision, so that even when one faces challenges on will be able to overcome.

NO ONE IS AN ISLAND; HAVE A MENTOR

If you're early on in your career, and given a choice between a great mentor and higher pay, take the mentor every time. It's not even close. Never think about leaving that mentor until you have acquired a substantial knowledge that can last you.

To be successful as a real estate investor, you must have it in mind that some people have done what you want to venture in. Approach successful investors that have a good reputation. To be successful, you have to learn from those who have gone through the same path you want to thread. Don't be an island. Humbly learn from successful real investors. Take time to know the pros and cons of them. With this, you would save enough energy and resources which accumulates from starting from scratch without good background knowledge of what you are venturing in.

CONSCIOUSLY GUARD YOUR INTEGRITY

As you experience changes and breakthroughs, know that integrity, honesty, and truth are the highest vibrating energies to guide you forward. Everything else will fall away. Molly McCord, Conscious Messages:

Integrity is tough to build and very easy to lose. The good name one has developed over a long period can be destroyed in a single deal if one does not take care. As a real estate investor chose your associate carefully. Do not associate with crooks or unnecessarily crafty people. Avoid this set of people:

-   Those that advice you only about the get-rich-quick schemes. They claim to be able to give you principles of making it without being hardworking. They encourage cutting corners, and usually, they lack any credentials or experience of real property investment.
-   People who can't offer success stories prove that they have been able to teach others their success principles.

One should not go into real estate investment with the view of making it at all cost even at the expense of other people. One right turn deserves another. A good estate investor must guide buyers rightly on suggested offer pricing; they should guide sellers on realistic home prices. Never provide a service that will ruin your reputation. To be a successful real estate investor, honesty, fairness, excellent communication, integrity, and diligence are needful.

Be Consistent and Hold Yourself Accountable

Real estate is not something you will become an expert overnight. What you can become an expert in immediately is your approach to each day. Be consistent. Write a list of items that you are going to accomplish at the beginning of each day and the end each day, hold yourself accountable. Commit to learning something new daily. It can range from further information about a community or understanding contracts better. Don't be afraid to ask questions. We were all new agents at one point, and many people willing to help.

BUILD YOUR NETWORK

To be a successful real estate agent, one must have a strong network that provides a steady source of business and referrals. So many people make the mistake of forgetting to maintain the relationships of their core network while focusing on creating new contacts. Though it is essential to growing, it is also necessary to keep all links. Since there is a lot of competition in real estate, one must join organizations where one can meet people who share your perception and business idea.

LEARN FROM YOUR MISTAKES

Never go to real estate investment with the mindset that you are infallible. Nobody is perfect. Instead of this, be collaborative. Learn to unlearn and relearn; Avoid mistake as much as you can, but much more importantly, making a mistake should not make you feel like a failure. What determines a crash is when you make a mistake, and you are not able to move past it and make a better decision in the future. For the fact that you screwed up in a previous deal should not be a psychological hindrance for future sale and opportunities.

Jack Canfield has this to say on learning from one's mistake that, "By taking the time to stop and appreciate who you are and what you've achieved - and perhaps learned through a few mistakes, stumbles, and losses - you actually can enhance everything about you. Self-acknowledgment and appreciation are what give you the insights and awareness to move forward toward higher goals and accomplishments".

ALL YOU NEED TO BE SUCCESSFUL IS YOU

- Kill your excuses and procrastination
- Destroy every form of distraction
- Avoid associating with negative minds. It is because they have a problem with every solution.
- Hang out with people who are more knowledgeable than you are.
- Build mutual relationships with those who are already where you want to be.
- Always feed your focus.
- Be patient and consistent in what you do.
- Add value to people's lives.

- Have a written goal and clearly define your purpose.
- Visualize where you want to be and be ready to pay the price to get there.

Many times, people will tell you that something is not going to work. It's your choice whether you listen to them, or prove them wrong. A negative mind will never give you a positive life! Success in life is the result of sound judgment. Good judgment is usually the result of experience. Experience is often the result of a bad review."

BE PATIENT AND CONSISTENT

Deontay Wilder's quote of all time is that 'Having patience is one of the hardest things about being human. We want to do it now, and we don't want to wait. Sometimes we miss out on our blessing when we rush things and do it on our own time. But in real estate, if you don't have patience enough, you will fizzle out and lose focus.

In real estate, one has to be patient. If you are not patient enough, one failure might make you give up. If you are not patient enough, you might be tempted to cut corners which will at the end of the day, be detrimental. To know more about patience in real estate meet up with successful investors with integrity there, you can learn their success story and consistency.

The reason most people not successful is because they lack the virtue of patience. They don't want to wait for their investment in developing. They want to watch it grow after the first week or month.

BUILD YOUR RESILENCE

Another mindset to put in place in real estate management is the focused mindset. Never be distracted. Stay focused on the need to be successful. Never jump from investment to another at the emergence of a difficulty. Lots of well-meaning people may offer supposedly good advice that might be a great hindrance to your dreams. They might try to tell you that real estate is not best for you. That does not mean they are right or wrong; all you need is to stay focused on your goal.

Unless they have more experience with making money in real estate than you or the person you're learning from, you should sieve their advice. Don't need to be rude. Appreciate then for their concern and explain to them why you know investing.

PURSUE KNOWLEDGE

Albert Einstein says he has no particular talent, and he is only passionately curious." One must not be tired of learning new things. Learn from people. Utilize the media. Learn from online stores on how to improve your real estate investment. With that one is updated and not out of tune with development in the actual property world.

DEFINE YOUR EARLY RETIREMENT DESTINATION

A CLEAR VIEW OF FINANCIAL INDEPENDENCE

Financial independence is when you can sustain the lifestyle you want based on the wealth you have accumulated. While you must be financially independent of retiring, you do not necessarily have to retire to be economically independent. In summary, financial independence is a height attained when work becomes an option. In another word, financial freedom is the art and science of having enough. Financial freedom is the status of having enough income to pay one's living expenses for the rest of one's life without having to be employed or dependant on others. Commonly referred to as passive income if one earns without having to work a job. What amounts to financial independence is the ability to generate revenue to meet one's needs from sources other than one's main job.

There are many strategies to achieve financial independence, each with their benefits and drawbacks. Making financial freedom will be helpful if one has a business plan and budget, to know what money is coming in and going out, have a clear view of the current incomes and expenses, and can identify and choose appropriate strategies to move towards one's financial goals. To feel productive, one must strive to make decisions that increase one's financial freedom. A business plan addresses every aspect of one's finances.

Financial independence is essential because one no longer relies on the paycheck to support one's life; it also helps in deciding how to live one's life with flexibility. The feeling that one's life its activities and habits are self-chosen and self endorsed is a contributory factor to happiness. Financial independence is excellent when one achieve it, but getting there takes time discipline and also in most cases requires sacrifices in lifestyle.

COMPONENTS OF FINANCIAL INDEPENDENCE

SAVING AND INVESTMENT

Investing is putting money to work to start or expand a project - or to purchase an asset or interest - where those funds are put to work, with the goal to income and increased value over time. The term "investment" can refer to any mechanism used for generating future income. In the financial sense, this includes the purchase of bonds, stocks, or real estate property among several others. Additionally, a constructed building or other facility used to produce goods seen as an investment. The production of products required to provide additional assets may also perceive as investing.

ESTATE PLANNING

Real estate investing involves the purchase, ownership, management, rental, and sale of real estate for profit. Improvement of realty property as part of a real estate investment strategy is generally considered to be a sub-specialty of real estate investing called real estate development. A real estate is an asset form with limited liquidity relative to other investments, it is also capital intensive (although money may gain through mortgage leverage) and is highly cash flow dependent. If these factors are not well understood and managed by the investor, real estate becomes a risky investment.

PAY DOWN DEBT

The basics for setting up your debt payment plan involve you writing down the amount you owe, the interest rate, and the minimum payment for each debt. Then list the obligations in the order you want to pay them off. You can do this from the highest interest rate to the lowest or from the smallest debt to the largest. You can use a debt calculator online or a service like Savvy Money that will help you see how quickly you can pay down the debt by increasing the amount you pay towards debt each month. The more you can apply to the liability, the faster you will be able to pay it off. Once you have worked hard to pay off your debts, you need to work hard to stay out of debt. It means you should continue to budget, and that you need to plan for the future. Setting up emergency funds and sinking funds should help you to deal with unexpected expenses and for car repairs. You will need to create a solid financial plan that plans for expenses like purchasing your first home and retirement. Although you may not want to continue paying attention to your budget, and your money.

RETIREMENT PLANNING

Retirement planning is the process of determining retirement income goals and the actions and decisions necessary to achieve those goals. Retirement planning includes identifying sources of income, estimating expenses, implementing a savings program, and managing assets and risk.

HOW MUCH WEALTH DO YOU NEED TO RETIRE USING REAL ESTATE

According to Benjamin Franklin, there are two ways to increase one's wealth. Increase your means and decrease your want. The best to do both at the same time.

INCREASE YOUR INCOME: there are different ways of increasing one's income through real estate. They include:

Cash Flow

Wise investors don't bet on appreciation. They purchase properties on a sound judgment that the property will generate more income than it costs to own. For these folks, who "cash flow" positively, they don't care what the market does. If prices drop, they are safe. If rates rise, they have more options.

Appreciation

That said, gratitude, or the rising of home prices over time, is how the majority of wealth builds in real estate. It is the "home run" you hear of when people make a massive windfall of money. While prices fluctuate, over the long-run real estate values have always gone up, ever, and there is no reason to think that is going to change.

Leverage

Leverage is such a critical part of real estate ownership that we often take it for granted. Where else can I borrow money from A (the bank), pay that loan back with payment from B (the tenant), and keep the difference for myself? The best way to get safe leverage is cash flow. If you make sure your property produces more income than it costs to own, the force itself doesn't matter as much. Those who "over leverage" property are those who borrow so much against it that they lose money every month.

GROW UR WEALTH

One has to increase both the value one provides and one's skill at turning a profit into money. You should not remain complacent at just one earning a level. You should always strive to improve your earnings.

DEVELOP YOUR BUSINESS POTENTIAL

One has to pick something and start. Never to be mindful of wrong decisions. When it comes to making money, it is pertinent to know that inaction is almost always worse than incorrect action. According to Henry Ford, ' one who fears failure limits his activities.

Failure is the only opportunity to move intelligently to begin again. There is no disgrace in honest failure. There is a disgrace in fearing to fail'. Wealth eludes most people because they are preoccupied with events, not taking into account the process that leads to the development of wealth. For every function of wealth are preceded by a long string process, a backpack of hardship, failures, tears, sacrifices

MATHEMATICS OF FINANCIAL INDEPENDENCE

FIGURE OUT YOUR EXPENSES

You should not override your savings. If expenses were higher, then the number is negative and represents a loss. Therefore, the formula for calculating net income is revenues subtract costs. Rearranging the equation, if we know total revenues and net income, we can calculate total costs by taking total revenues and subtracting net income.

APPLY THE 4% RULE:

Right from time, financial experts use the 4% rule to know how much to save for retirement and what kind of and what type of annual income retirement savings would provide. William Bengen propounded the Government in the 1990s. The law provides that if retirees withdraw 4% of their savings annually, their nest egg, I.e., money saved is used in the future, will last at least 30 years. There is a rule of thumb, based on studies looking at historical stock market returns, that states you can withdraw approximately 4% of the initial value of your portfolio, year after year, over long periods without running out of money. There is no guarantee that future market returns will ensure

45

the 4% rule persists, but it's a reasonable approximation. For this exercise, take the estimated annual expenses you determined in step #1 and multiply them by 25. It is roughly the size of the investment portfolio required for you to achieve financial independence, assuming there are no contributions from other income sources, such as rental property, a pension, or social security.

CHOOSE YOUR RETIREMENT AGE AND CALCULATE HOW MUCH YOU NEED TO SAVE

Next, decide at what age you would like to become financially independent and assume a rate of return for your investments. It will allow you to calculate the amount you must save each year toward the goal of financial independence.

When thinking about what rate of return to use, keep in mind that stocks have historically produced real returns of approximately 7% annually, while bonds have returned around 2% annually. A real return is simply the investment return of a stock or bond, minus inflation. Depending on what percent of your investments you plan to put in stocks versus bonds, your assumed rate of return will vary along the 2-7% spectrum. While future returns are never guaranteed, for our purposes, we will use 5% as a reasonable assumption.

CRITERIA FOR ATTAINING ONE's EARLY RETIREMENT DESTINATION

PLAN THE FUTURE

Thinking long-term is an essential characteristic of accumulating wealth and achieving financial independence. There can be several considerations for long-term wealth, and they will differ for everyone.

If you are a doctor or lawyer, you need to put in long hours after years of specialty training and higher education to get a paycheck. However, in any occupation, as discussed, your annual salary does not necessarily translate to wealth. With long-term thinking, helping to ensure your job's security, taking the initiative to achieve a promotion, or taking steps that will result in higher sales commissions can all be factors for wealth and ways to help ease your anxieties over financial independence.

Side gigs, private investments, and a host of other variables also utilize for long-term thinking, wealth accumulation, and achieving financial independence. A few considerations here may include a portfolio of private businesses, car washes, parking garages, stocks, bonds, mutual funds, real estate, patents, and trademarks. Some of these cash generators can be relied on for long-term income in addition to your job or just as cash generators that can pull in money while you take long vacations or sit by the pool.

KEEP THE BALANCE SHEET GREEN

When you take a look at your balance sheet, you may already have organic investments; you can rely on in your quest for financial independence. Often, this is wealth that generates capital gains, income, and dividends without labor. The more of these investments you can afford, the sooner you can fully achieve financial independence.

SET ACHIEVABLE GOALS

Overall, the real value of your income is partially determined by the amount you can invest to achieve a financial independence goal. Setting this goal can be essential for keeping your perspective on income in check. At your goal, you can successfully maintain the lifestyle you want without working.

PLAN YOUR TIME

Having complete control over your time is often one factor in achieving financial independence.

If you find the profession that gives you that feeling,

and you are disciplined in your management of the business side of it by controlling costs, you have a massive advantage over your competition because you may continue to work for a long time, not because you need to, but because you love the process and product itself

GET GOING

According to Robert Kiyosaki in his book, Rich Dad, Poor Dad, he explained the reason why people with 'A' grade work for people with 'C' grade. If you want to guess who is going to be wealthy and financially independent, you'd be more likely finding a self-sufficient person who paid for his car, gets decent (but not spectacular) grades, has a job and enjoys what he does than selecting someone from the honor roll. It's counterintuitive, but it's often true.

RELATIONSHIPS

You must associate with the person who has the same financial goal with you. If you marry someone who spends extravagantly, he might end up pulling down you dream of attaining financial independence. If you are successful and your spouse is equally disciplined, frugal, and investment-oriented, your efforts toward a better, financially independent life are going to be like harness, productive and realistic

REAL ESTATE INVESTING STRATEGIES EXPLAINED

BUY AND HOLD

If you are thinking of a long term investment strategy in real estate, then buy and hold is the way to go. It is an investing strategy with an exceptional array of advantages.

Due to the amount of time involved in this strategy, you must do your research correctly and create a fail-proof business strategy.

In the innate sense of it, buy and hold involves long term rental properties. The right hires and holds real estate can yield both short term gains and long term appreciation.

When you buy and hold real estate, you buy a property and hold on to it for an extended period. Often, the goal is to sell the real estate, but the property can be rented out before the grand scale, which is where the short term gains come in.

When considering buy and hold real estate strategy, it is essential to calculate the potential income generate by renting out the property. The investor must ensure that the monthly income should be more than the monthly expenses the property will accrue. Expenses the investor considers include:

- Mortgage payments
- Interest
- Taxes
- Fees
- Maintenance costs

Consider the potential profit after the final sale. An investor must also factor in the price of taking out loans or other types of financing.

HOUSE FLIPPING

House flipping may relate to real-time trading in real estate. As with trading, any bought property with the intent to flip must be purchased with quick reselling. The time between the purchase and the sale is not fixed as it often ranges from a couple of months up to a year.

There are two different types of house flipping:

- Buying a property that has the potential to increase in value with the right repairs. After completing the work, the property sells at a higher price than acquired.
- I am buying a property in a market where the features are rapidly rising in values. The

property is held for a few months, then resold at a higher price and profit is made.

While flipping a house may sound simple, but it's not as easy as it looks. A house flip can go either way. A house flip can be an excellent investment if done the right way. But a house flip can just as quickly go the wrong direction if done the wrong way. A house flip may not make you money. It actually could cost you thousands. Here are a few tips to ensure you don't end up investing in what will eventually tie your money down with no hope for getting the capital back, talk less of making a profit:

Financing the house flip

Flipping a house with debt is a risky move because the entire house flipping process is a risk. Endorsement that you flip a home with cash is encouraged because investors who borrow for their purchase pay interest for months. Therefore, they have to increase the amount they have to sell the house in order even to get their capital back.

Also, investors who take out a loan to flip a house might act rashly and sell the house at a cheap rate to prevent the interest from accruing over time. A Cash-only flipper can wait for a time when the property is sold at a premium. Unless you can pay cash, the financial risk of house flipping is not worth it.

Get to know the Market

If you don't have a good understanding of the real estate market, you can run into some issues. To start with, you must have done your homework and be familiar with the market value of a property you intend to flip. Your best bet is to buy such property at 70% of market value AFTER you have subtracted the cost of repairs.

There's no way you can tell what the exact potential value of the property is so you have to factor in your vision for property as well as the neighborhood it is located in to arrive at the final figure. Now, say houses in the region are usually sold within the range of a hundred thousand to one-fifty, the price of your flip should ideally within the lower end of the spectrum when it's ready for sale.

To get a deep understanding of the market that makes for a successful flip, find a real estate agent with years of experience in your area. With the aid of the agent, you can get the right house in the right neighborhood that will allow you to make a profit when your vision for the home has been executed.

Imagine this scenario: you get a house for $125K in a neighborhood where the most expensive homes go for $150K, but you didn't know this because you did not find out. You spend $30K on repairs and updates and eventually, you want to sell the house for $180K, but no one is buying. You have a liability on your hands!

Working with a real estate agent who knows the market like the back of their hand is the best way to make a smart investment that keeps your finances on track.

Have a Budget

Prepare a budget right from the start such that you already know how much you will purchase the home, the cost of repairs and renovations as well as the rice you intend to sell before you venture into house flipping at all.

Identify everything you need to repair and construct in the house to prevent surprise repairs, which can make or break a flip.

Invest in Smart Renovations

Have a plan for the parts of the house you intend to renovate and then stick to that list alone. Make sure your updates stay on track and boost the value of the home.

Significant renovations like kitchens and bathrooms can easily make or break your flip.

Consider smarter renovation that ensures that you'll spend less while having a higher likelihood of recouping your costs. The power of small tweaks should never be underestimated. Things like a fresh coat of paint, updated hardware, and new landscaping can make a massive difference in the price you eventually sell your products.

WHOLESALE REAL ESTATE

Commercial real estate involves finding a great real estate deal and then selling it to another party interested in the transaction.

When it comes to real estate investing, there's more than one way to go about it. Wholesaling allows you to put the leveraging power of a good deal to work for you to make money with little-to-nothing in a contract, no financing, and no repair work or landlord duties.

You are not selling the property; you are the middle-person selling them your position in the contract. You are not looking to make money from the property itself, but rather on the deal by collecting a fee from another interested investor.

There are many advantages to wholesaling real estate.

Usually, the only money you put into wholesale is your earnest money. Thankfully, this is entirely negotiable with the seller, and it can be as little as a few hundred dollars. Almost anyone can afford that. And if you negotiate your contract correctly, you have virtually no risk to lose that money should the deal go south.

Because you don't try to close the property in wholesaling, but rather try and sell the contract to another buyer, there is no need for a loan. It's just the escrow fee you put up.

Finally, you don't have to worry about being a landlord and doing repairs on the property or maintenance. Because you're never technically the owner of the property, but rather the owner of a great deal in the form of a contract, you don't have to spend any time or money doing the regular upkeep and repairs that a landlord would have to.

STEPS TO TAKE

Find the right property.

The best properties for wholesale deals usually are

distressed properties of some kind. They can be abandoned houses that need a lot of repairs, perhaps owned by a bank and up for foreclosure. Do a simple internet search to find them.

Properties that have been on the market for a long time are also excellent for this deal. Owners get more desperate as time goes on, paying a mortgage for a house they don't live in. Use the internet to look for deals in your area that have been on the market for many months.

Use keywords like "motivated," "must sell," "fixer-upper," "as is," and more to find the right kinds of deals that would work in wholesaling.

Run the numbers

You aim to sell a contract, not a property, so you want to take different costs into account to make sure your fee is substantial for your work.

Costs to consider include, title fees, any fees you might put out to have a contractor evaluate needed repairs, and the services of an appraiser. The goal is to know how much you need to put up for the deal and what you think you can sell the contract for. The difference between the two is your net fee. Typically, you'll want your payment to be $2,000 or more, depending on how great the deal is. If you're not going to make that much on the sale, then it's not worth doing.

Find the owner

Find a way to contact the owner. If the contact details for the owner aren't in the listings you're looking at, you can go to the neighbors, knock on the door, and ask if they know the owner. Often they can give you a phone number or email to connect with.

Negotiate the contract

The key to success in wholesaling is to negotiate a great deal. The better the agreement, the easier it is to find an investor and make a high fee.

The name of the game in commercial real estate investing is margin. The larger the potential profit margin for your eventual buyer, the better your fee will be. You must give yourself an escape clause.

Any number of problems can arise, such as the property not passing an inspection, and the property does not appraise for high enough of value or title issues. Write the contract in a way that provides exit opportunities for these situations. Use as few escape clauses as possible, but have at least one phrase to get out of the deal.

Find your buyer

Once you have your contract negotiated and signed, the clock starts to tick for you to find the right buyer for the deal. Your best bet is to sell to an investor because they are always in the market for a great deal. Here are a few ways to find one:

- Advertising online, flyers or Newspapers
- Real estate investing clubs
- Networking at foreclosure auctions

In commercial real estate, you have to build your database of interested real estate investors. Be on the lookout for names to add to your database so that when the time comes, all you have to do is go through your list to find a buyer quickly and you get to have a lot of choices. Investors are different. Take the time to find out what each one of them is looking for before you have a contract in place. That way, you know to send exclusive deals to those who would be most interested.

Once you find the right buyer for the contract, you will both go to your title company's office where the agreement will be assigned to the buyer, the deal completed, and the title transferred to the investor.

N.B: Find a title company that understands how real estate wholesaling works to ensure the closing goes smoothly.

REAL ESTATE DEVELOPMENT

In real estate development, you buy land, finance real estate deals, and build projects from scratch. It involves a lot of risks but has the potential to yield great rewards.

To be a successful real estate developer, you must be able to deliver properties that will improve quality of life for those who live in such houses. Most developers focus on building wealth that easily adapts to clients' needs regardless of whether they are single professionals, older adults, or a family.

Efficient real estate development is dependent on a strong relationship with lawyers, bankers, architects, tenants, general contractors, surveyors, civil engineers, and existing tenants. Creativity is essential here, and an average performance will not cut it. A developer must be able to think into the future and see what type of properties will be well accepted by clients.

If you are not good at tolerating risks, this might not be the niche for you. There is a possibility that things might not go the way you envisioned. To be successful here, you have to take calculated risks and be able to mitigate such risks. This requires a unique skill set and experience.

HOUSE HACKING

House Hacking is a real estate investment strategy where investors rent out portions of their home to generate income that is used to pay off some of the costs associated with owning a home. The challenge with this is that the owner must be willing to take on a little more work and sacrifice some comforts.

Here are the potential benefits of this strategy:

- Acquire extra tax write-offs leading to a reduction in your mortgage interest.
- Generate revenue by renting out parts of your property.
- It is decreasing transportation costs like gas.
- Learn how to be a landlord and become a real estate investor.

With House Hacking, you don't have to put down 20-25% of the property's value when you buy. You can buy a home with very low or no money down because it is meant to be used as your primary residence.

Over the past decade, housing has become too expensive for most home buyers to afford comfortably. However, instead of moving miles away from where you work or renting an apartment, you can buy properties and have others pay a large part of the expenses.

The best way to do this is to buy multiple unit buildings that have spaces with which you can generate revenue. The icing on the cake is that you can buy such properties with a low down payment.

When analyzing a property as a potential House Hack opportunity, look for the following features:

-   Anything that is two units or more is a plus, with more units being better than less. The goal of House Hacking is to lower your payment as much as possible, not to buy the prettiest house. The neighborhood where they are located is essential. You're better off buying multi-family properties in communities where they are mixed in with the single-family properties. This encourages fewer investors to flood the area with tenants and usually improves home values.
-   Finished basement that has been converted into separate living areas
-   Additional Dwelling Units

- Multiple Bedroom Houses
- Areas Easily Converted to Bedrooms
- Houses Near Public Transportation
- Home Owner Associations allow for non-owner occupancy and short term rentals (like Airbnb).
- Adequate parking spaces
- Safe neighborhoods where property crimes are low,
- Areas that tenants want to live.
- Houses With Adequate Living Space allow your tenants to live comfortably.
- Bigger houses with extra bathrooms and multiple bedrooms make the best House Hack Opportunities.

SHORT TERM RENTALS

Short term rentals are also called vacation rentals. The owners rent out their properties on a nightly or weekly basis to people who are searching for and book accommodations.

The offer is listed on Airbnb or other home-sharing platforms and online community marketplaces. This is a growing real estate market mainly due to the privacy and space a short-term rental offers to tenants.

As an owner of a vacation home, you will need a short-term rental license to be able to rent it out. A renting license reassures your guest that he will be safe in your home.

Check the protected areas for this business based on your location with local authorities.

If you want to make a profit out of your second apartment or a vacation house best idea is to work with a short-term rental management firm to help you rent and advertise.

Vacation rental insurance is a crucial step to make before renting out your property. It covers not only the possible property damages but also the accidents that the guest might suffer while staying there. The property owner could direct the guest to the insurance company to sign for travel insurance. In either case, it is mandatory that everyone is covered with the right type of insurance.

LIVE-IN HOUSE FLIPS

An investor interested in Do-It-Yourself projects will have a swell time with this type of house flip. A live-in flip involves the investor residing in a primary residence while fixing it up and selling it to get the profit of the flip typically after two years. A two year period is optimal because living in a primary residence for two years allows the investor the opportunity to not pay taxes on the capital gains from the sale of the house up to an amount. The capital tax gains would not work unless it's a primary residence, so this would not work for a buy and flip investment. The pros of life in house flips start with the cost of living, which are considerably lessened because the investor is living in the project instead of paying for living arrangements as well as the mortgage for the flip.

By doing this, it is possible to cut costs in half since the two values are now combined.

Imagine this scenario:

You have a monthly housing cost of $2000

Your flip monthly mortgage is $1500 holding cost

That's a total of $3500 per month for the total number of months it will take you to complete renovations and upgrades.

If it's a Live-in flip, all you have to pay is a monthly mortgage of $1000, and your monthly housing is entirely free!

However, there are cons to it. If as an investor, you cannot stand living in the middle of a construction zone, then that's a problem. If you are not a DIY person, you will have to hire contractors. They are a faster route but do come with a price which is bound to cut into your profit down the line.

The advantages of a live-in flip are numerous, and it would be perfect for anyone interested in flipping houses. Also, there are rehab budget advantages to this style as compared to the traditional buy and flip-style. You can use your credit cards to get construction materials on low monthly payments compared to the entire cost of your rehab budget

THE BRRRR (BUY, REHAB, RENT, REFINANCE, REPEAT) STRATEGY

Buy

The goal behind a BRRRR strategy is to pull all of the money you put into a property out when you refinance it so that you effectively bought a property for nothing, but still have 25 percent built-in equity to reduce risk.

To purchase the property upfront, you can use cash, a hard money loan, seller financing, a private loan, etc.

Different upfront financing options will result in the different acquisition and holding costs

Rehab

There are two key questions to keep in mind when rehabbing a rental:

What do I need to do to make this house livable and functional?

Which rehab decisions can I make that will add more value than their cost?

Specific rehabs cost much more than the property value they will produce. They include: Granite Countertops, Skylights, Hot Tubs, Chandeliers, etc

It's also rarely worth finishing a basement or a garage when it comes to rentals. Practical rehabs like two-tone paint refinished hardwoods, and adding tile are very often worthwhile.

The house needs to be in good shape, and everything needs to be functional. You must strike that delicate balance between renting excellent properties and rehabbing with luxury items which will cost you more than get back.

Rent

Screen carefully to ensure that you get tenants that will pay each month. Notify the tenant that you are doing an appraisal beforehand. They don't need to be present, but you should ask them to clean up and keep any pets if they aren't home.

Refinance

When looking for banks willing to refinance, do not just jump into the arms of the first bank you find. Ask the following questions first:

Do they offer cash out or will they only pay off debt? If they don't offer money out, you will probably want to move on.

What seasoning period do they require?

A "seasoning period" is how long you have to own a property before the bank lends on the appraised value instead of how much money you have into the park. For the BRRRR strategy to work, you need to borrow on the estimated value. These days, some banks are willing to lend on the assessed value as soon as a property has been rehabbed and rented. These are the best banks to find. The biggest challenge you should be prepared for is finding a lender that has less than a year seasoning period.

The most effective way to find such banks is to ask around. If a bank is lending to another investor, there is a good chance they will give to you, too.

Repeat

Repeat the process all over again!

THE PROBLEM WITH NO MONEY DOWN

Buying real estate with nothing out of pocket is possible. Money is still required, but other people's money is used rather than your own. But just because you can do it doesn't mean that you should. There are many creative ways to finance real estate. Some ideas will get you in trouble, but most are entirely legal and sometimes very ingenious.

One of the favored methods among real estate investors is to use seller financing. This strategy is most often used when accumulating rental properties or longer-term holds. Usually, the seller owns the home "free and clear" (no mortgage), but it is not necessary.

Instead of selling the home outright, the seller becomes the mortgage holder. Title to the house is passed to the buyer, but a mortgage or deed of trust is registered on the property with a promissory note where the buyer agrees to whatever terms were negotiated. This is a private transaction so pretty much any interest rate and/or points could be charged as long as both parties agree. Sellers may require a down payment, but if they don't, then you have yourself a no-money-down deal.

Another popular way to achieve no money down the deal is to use private money. This can be a wealthy friend or family member, or it can be a professional private lender or hard money lender. These people are not hard to find if you know where to look.

The problem with no money down deals is that interest payments can kill the cash flow and eat up profits. Investors can end up overpaying for a property because they wanted to keep their money out of the deal so badly that they didn't keep their eye on the bigger picture. Some people say price doesn't matter if investors can get the interest rate, payoff term, and down payment they want. While that statement is true to a degree, it certainly has its limitations.

As an investor, you need to think cash flow first, then ensure overall profitability of the deal and have at least two exit strategies. If these three crucial things cannot be reasonably assured, then you need to walk away regardless of the size of the down payment

REAL ESTATE INVESTING MYTHS

Here are the most commonly known real estate investing myths debunked.

Real estate investment is a quick and easy way to make money: By getting more real estate knowledge and learning how to invest in real estate, you will see that there is a high chance of success in the business. However, there is no quick and easy way to make money in real estate. Patience and determination to succeed are of utmost importance to make it. You must also invest time and effort to make a profit.

You need to have a lot of money to start investing: You do not have to finance your real estate deals all on your own. You can have a partner with whom to fund. If that is not a viable option for you, you can invest in cheaper properties such as fix-and-flips or become a wholesaler.

You must own a home before financing rental properties: Investing in real estate can kick-start the process of funding of your property. Imagine that you receive a monthly rent of $4,000 on the single-family property. Meanwhile, you live in a park with $1,500 rent, and you pay $1,500 as a mortgage. You are paying off your rent and mortgage from proceeds on your property and also making a neat profit off it.

You do not need to be a licensed real estate agent before becoming a real estate investor. These two phenomena can be mutually exclusive. It is not compulsory that a real estate investor simply because you are an agent. In the same vein, you do not need to be a real estate agent to become a housing investor. It is not a necessity to be licensed to start investing in real estate. There is a wide array of information to be learned online. Also, the more you practice, the better you will get.

Some people will have you believe that a real estate is a passive form of investment. That is not entirely true. There are investing strategies that bring passive income to the investor, and they still require some involvement. For example, when renting out a multi-family home or a single-family home long term, the investor technically receives a passive income. However, a lot of effort went into securing that property in the first place, and the property must also be maintained. Taking a backseat is a sure way to lose your capital.

Invest in a real estate close to your own home: There are benefits to this, such as familiarity with the market, ease of keeping an eye on the property and avoiding travel costs. However, if you want to be making money in real estate, you should not put such limits.

Real estate market analysis is not necessary: On the contrary, it is a must if you want to be making money in real estate. It might be a challenging thing to do on your own, but some tools can help you. This is where rental property calculators come in.

HOW TO AND WHY USE OTHER PEOPLE'S MONEY(OPM) TO INVEST IN REAL ESTATE

Investing with other people's money gives an investor the opportunity to pay for real estate investment opportunities privately lending money from a bank. Private lenders are most often silent partners that have the money to invest in real estate to benefit from the financial return without the time or interest in doing the work of real estate investing. In the process of building your real estate investing network, you must focus a great deal on growing your private lender options.

HOW TO USE OPM IN REAL ESTATE INVESTMENT

Seller financing

Here, the seller keeps the mortgage in their name. The investor then makes payments to the seller to cover the monthly mortgage payment. An arrangement is made so that the investor has rights to the property, including the right to sell the property for a profit.

Equity partner

The equity partner is also known as a cash investor. For some investment opportunities, the investor can get multiple equity partners to create a pool of money for the investment. Cash investors receive either a percentage of the return on the real estate deal or interest with repayment.

Land Contract

The seller holds the title until conditions of the contract are fulfilled by the buyer.

Subject To

The existing mortgage stays in place, but the title is transferred to the new buyer

WHY USE OPM FOR REAL ESTATE INVESTING

As a new investor, your access to cash is limited. Private funding is a great way to build your investment scope as well as your cash reserves for future investment opportunities.

Your risk and exposure are limited when you use other people's money. With real estate investing, chances are a constant threat. However, when you use other people's money, you limit your risks while both you and your private lender have the potential to see positive gains. To have long-term success, however, you must be serious about your investments. If you get a reputation for losses, it'll be challenging to continue finding funding options.

RAISING PRIVATE MONEY TO FUND YOUR DEALS

Private money can be a powerful tool to fund real estate investment deals. As a new investor, raising private money for real estate is no easy task. It will require that you put in a lot of hard work and time. Once your portfolio picks up and starts to grow, getting funding becomes easier. Raising private money at the beginning, may be harder; therefore, the following tips will come handy:

Use your circle and expand it.

Talk to people who already have a relationship with you. It may surprise you how willing to help the people you already know maybe if you reach out. In addition to that, always attend local real estate club meetings and networking meetings to gain a trustworthy reputation.

Tell everyone you're a real estate investor and that you have a real estate investing business. Make sure everyone in your circle know about your business. Find ways to slip it into every conversation and do not make assumptions about who can or cannot help you invest.

Document details carefully.

By documenting the details of each transaction, you ensure that you have something to present to private lenders. Having detailed documentation of your previous deals help them see that you are a safe investment. Beyond that, you can also quickly tell how much you need to fund a new contract based on your track record. Being detail-oriented also shows potential lenders that you are mindful of your business.

Invest in your own money.

By using your own money, you will be forced to consider every decision carefully and be proactive with your strategies. Thus, you know the exact amount of funding you need in the future. Involving your own money will also show potential lenders that you have a substantial stake in the investment and improve your investment rep.

Look for opportunities to teach people about private lending.

By doing this, you are positioned as an expert, and potential lenders trust experts. They get the sense that their investment is secure with you because of Expert!

It can also help you find new private lenders. By explaining the benefits of private lending compared with traditional forms of investing, you'll surely pique their interest.

Flaunt your success

Do not be afraid to talk about deals you've brokered successfully. Put them on social media and share them at networking events. Draw attention to yourself as a successful investor. It's a great way to get lenders interested in you.

Focus on building solid relationships

Build relationships with people who will help you find private money and improve your real estate investment career in the long run.

WHAT IS PRIVATE MONEY AND WHO ARE PRIVATE LENDERS?

Private Lenders issue short-term loans for the purchase and/or renovation of an investment property. They're commonly known as "hard money lenders." They offer private money loans to short-term and long-term investors looking for quick funding. They can be anyone from a personal friend to an established private lending company.

When investors speak of private lenders, they're usually referring to hard money lenders. This is because hard money lenders issue short-term real estate loans used to purchase and renovate an investment property.

Technically, there are three degrees of private lenders based on the relationship between the borrower and the lender.

- Primary circle (family and friends)
- Secondary circle (Colleagues and acquaintances)
- Third-party loop (Accredited investors and hard money lenders)

Hard money lenders are considered to be "third-party" private lenders. They are the ones with whom the borrower has the least involvement with in terms of a relationship. In spite of this, hard money lenders are the best private lenders because they're the most reliable and most standardized.

Private money lenders are right for investors looking to purchase, renovate, and sell a property within a year. Long-term investors who need financing quickly can also use private money lenders. Private lenders often issue loans to short-term investors looking to make money flipping houses. They also issue both rehab loans as well as traditional hard money loans to buy-and-hold investors looking to purchase and/or renovate a rental property.

As earlier discussed, private lenders can be different types of people. Therefore, the rates and terms of a private money loan can vary widely.

Hard money lenders usually offer private money loans up to:

90% of a property's loan to value (LTV)

80% of a property's after repair value (ARV)

A property's LTV ratio is a loan amount based on a percentage of its initial purchase price, similar to a conventional mortgage. A property's ARV ratio is a loan amount based on the expected fair market value

(FMV) of an estate after renovations are completed.

Private money borrowers pay monthly interest throughout the term of the loan and then make full repayment at the end of the loan. Some lenders charge prepayment penalties if the loan is paid off before the due date while most don't let you pay early and reduce your holding costs.

Interest rates can vary between 7% to 13%

Private money loans are an excellent option for buy and flip investors who want to reduce their holding costs while preparing a property for sale. It is also a good deal for buy-and-hold investors since the monthly payments don't cost much.

Look out for the following when looking for a private money lender:

A lender who has done more than 100 deals.

Work with a hard money lender who is an expert in the type of property you're looking to finance.

Be on the lookout for the lowest available interest rates and fees for a private loan.

Work with a lender that doesn't have a prepayment penalty, hence giving the borrower more repayment options.

THE ELEVATOR PITCH

Imagine this scenario:

You are a fresh real estate investor, but your portfolio is multiplying, and you are working on a new investment. You are in the process of acquiring a property that is perfect for a quick flip, and you walked into a former client. After exchanging pleasantries, he asks you what you've been up to. You are assailed by all the information in your head, but you have no idea where to start. You start to speak, but then you pause. Your thoughts are not organized, and you're struggling to put two and two together. Just then, he/she receives an urgent phone call, and they have to leave.

You just missed a one in a million chance to get a much-needed investor! If you'd been better prepared, there is a 100% chance they would have stayed long enough to schedule a meeting. This could have been prevented if you had an "elevator pitch."

The elevator pitch is a short rehearsed speech that explains what you do without mincing words. An effective elevator pitch is brief, persuasive and it sparks interest. It should not last any longer than 20 to 30 seconds, the amount of time it takes to complete an elevator ride. It should be witty and must explain what makes your investment idea extraordinary.

Creating an Elevator Pitch

It can take some time to get your pitch right. You'll likely go through several versions before finding compelling one, and that sounds natural in conversation. Follow these steps to create a high pitch, but you must vary your approach based on what your tone is about.

1. Identify Your Goal

Start by thinking about the objective of your pitch. For instance, if your goal is to tell a potential client about a house you have recently renovated and are preparing to flip, you must talk about the house succinctly and ensure that you sell its strong points. Talk about nothing else but this. Identify and focus on your goal

2. Explain What You Do

Start your pitch by describing what you do. Focus on the problems that you solve and how you help people. If you can, add information about how your property can help your potential client make money.

Keep in mind that your pitch should excite you first; after all, if you don't get excited about what you're saying, neither will your audience. Your pitch should bring a smile to your face and quicken your heartbeat. People may not remember everything that you say, but they will likely remember your enthusiasm.

Example:

Imagine that you're creating an elevator pitch that describes what your real estate investment portfolio in a bid to get private money. You plan to use it at a real estate networking event. You could say, "I buy and flip properties."

That's not something that will catch people's attention. It is not a memorable statement. But if you tell them about the strengths of this property you intend to flip, such as the updates you have made and how it will benefit your potential client, then they will listen.

A better explanation would be, "I have a multi-unit family house that has recently been renovated and updated with state of the art fittings up for sale. It is located in the heart of Manhattan and costs lower than most of the houses you will find in that axis. It is a huge chance to invest as it will be worth double the current price in the next ten years."

That's much more interesting and shows the value that you are providing to potential clients.

3. Let your unique selling proposition shine

Your elevator pitch needs to communicate your unique selling proposition. In other words, you must identify what makes your idea unique. Communicate your USP after you've talked about what you do.

4. Engage With a question

After you communicate your USP, you need to engage your audience. To do this, prepare open-ended questions (questions that can't be answered with a "yes" or "no" answer) to involve them in the conversation.

Make sure that you're able to answer any questions that he or she may have.

5. Put It All Together

When you've completed each section of your pitch, put it all together.

Then, read it aloud and use a stopwatch to time how long it takes. It should be no longer than 20-30 seconds. Your pitch needs to be snappy and compelling, so the shorter it is, the better!

6. Practice

Like anything else, practice makes perfect. Remember, how you say it is just as important as what you say. If you don't practice, you'll likely talk too fast, sound unnatural, or forget essential elements of your pitch.

Set a goal to practice your pitch regularly. The more you practice, the more natural your ball will become. You want it to sound like a quiet conversation, not an aggressive sales pitch.

Make sure that you're aware of your body language as you talk, which conveys just as much information to the listener as your words do. Practice in front of a mirror or, better yet, in front of colleagues until the pitch feels natural.

HOW TO TALK TO POTENTIAL PRIVATE LENDERS

A significant determinant of getting a definite "yes" from a private lender is how well you communicate and how much credibility you have built with the person. Effective communication plays a significant role in whether or not you can convince your private lender to do business with you. Real estate interests a lot of people, they like the sound of it but often let their fear get in the way of going for it. That is where you come in; in this field, you position yourself as an expert who can help them make the most of their money they have eyed for so long without daring to break into.

As earlier discussed, talk about what you do as often as possible. Nobody will know you are a real estate investor if you do not talk about it. This is the ice breaker you need to get them interested and delve into more fruitful conversations.

Once there is someone interested in investing with you, it is your job to sell your value and the deal to them.

To begin with, you must have a fair understanding of what interested the person in the first place so you can determine how to position the deal to them.

Say, for instance, a member of your secondary circle consistently talks about making money; you should talk more about the returns and the money that they will build on the deal than about the actual property.

If they seem to be more interested in doing deals without the risk of their neck on the line, you should talk about your track record the safety of your investments.

Spend the first ten minutes of a meeting, or general conversation with a potential private lender on building rapport and creating a common ground upon which they can relate with you. Show genuine interest in their responses, make them feel important (because they ARE important to you), and focus on their mannerisms so you can mirror them.

Find out if they've ever done any private lending so you can determine their level of understanding and how much you need to explain to them.

You also need to know about their current investments to get an idea of where their money is currently located.

Typical interest rates for private lenders can fall anywhere between 8-12% interest, but this depends on the lender, the deal, their experience level, your experience level, the time frame, and so on. IT IS NEGOTIABLE.

Do not be a pushover. You are providing them with an opportunity. Remember the documentation of the details of your past transactions? Find a way to slip this in to give the assurance that you know what you are doing so the lender feels confident investing their money with you.

Prepare the following, so your lenders can feel safe with leaving their money with you:

- Promissory Note which states the terms of the agreement, the interest rate, time frames, etc.
- Deed of Trust is a mortgage from the lender to you.
- Hazard Insurance provides protection for the lender. Such that if the property were to burn to the ground, the private lender is listed as the person who would be paid back.
- Personal Guarantee shows your level of commitment to the deal. It is your legal promise that if you cannot repay this specific loan, you are held personally liable.

MEETING WITH YOUR POTENTIAL PRIVATE LENDER

Having access to capital can open many doors in the real estate investing business. Many new investors are intimidated at the thought of sitting down with a private money group and asking them for money. As a result, they will delay or postpone meetings, causing their business to suffer the consequences. However, there is no reason to fear such a meeting. Private money lenders want to work with you just as bad as you want to work with them. The initial assembly may be awkward, but there are things you can say, or do, that will give you a huge advantage. With the right moves, you will be able to secure the appropriate funding to make everyone money.

The most important thing you can do whenever you meet any potential contact is to be prepared. While obvious, you need to spend the time to think about every possible way the conversation may go. Hard money and private money lenders are focused on returns, but they also want to get a feel for who they are working with. In many cases, how you present yourself is just as important as what you will do with their money. The most significant cause for hesitation in asking for money is a lack of experience. Fortunately, a small track-record can be offset by a pleasant personality and substantial preparation.

Even if you have never worked with a private money lender before, you should put yourself in their shoes and think about their potential risks. Anyone lending money, whether it is a bank or a private money lender, is worrying about repayment and return. Before you start talking about specific deals, you need to get your finances in order. Debt-to-income ratios and the ability to show your income isn't nearly as big a deal to private money lenders, but they still need reassurances that you can pay their note in the event the rehab takes longer than expected, or other issues come up.

As you are preparing for the meeting, get any financial and current portfolio information ready. The more you have, the better you look.

Finances aside, private money lenders want to know how and when they will get their money back. If you have a track record, you can cite specific examples, but even if you don't, you can illustrate how you would operate if you did have access to money. The more specific and detailed you are, the better chance you have at getting money. It is a good idea to run your plans by a fellow investor or someone in the business that you trust. Try to find as many holes in your plan as possible and be prepared to address them. There are many ways to find deals and handle rehab projects. If you are confident in your method, you need to convey it. If you are questioned at your meeting and easily change your mind, you come across as someone who would wilt under pressure.

It is a good idea to bring a few potential deals to the meeting and discuss how you would work them and what you would use the money for. You will probably be asked how you plan on getting deals and what your methods of lead generation are. This is not a time to be coy and keep any Realtor or other network contacts to yourself. Your private money lender has to be an ally. The more they trust you, the more freedom you will have to act quickly and get more deals. If you can bring an agreement to the meeting that you can close and turnaround in 30 days, you will gain immediate credibility, and most likely a blank check for future business.

While private money meetings are a severe matter, there are ways to make them more personal. After all, real estate is a people business. You need to find opportunities to break the mood and show a sense of humor. Feel out the respective lender and establish a working relationship. If they can leave the meeting feeling that they know you and what you are about, it will make them think they can trust you. If they can trust you, they will most likely lend their money to you. It is OK to break the ice and talk about your family, what sports teams you like, or any other current news item. You should know which areas to stay away from, particularly controversial issues, but you do need to lighten up the mood and show some of your personality. Lenders lend based on numbers, but they also give based on nature.

Not every first meeting will end in a relationship. Sometimes it may not be a good fit, or the timing might not be significant. This doesn't mean you shouldn't follow up and stay in contact. You never know when the right deal will come along. A successful private money lender meeting can change your business for the better. If you are prepared, it should go well.

THE LEGAL ASPECTS OF RAISING MONEY FROM PRIVATE INVESTORS

Securities Laws

"The Securities Act of 1933 was enacted in the wake of the stock market crash in the 1930s after many investors lost money to investment "Promoters" who promised returns that were never realized. The government subsequently passed laws to protect investors from unscrupulous sponsors. The new rules defined what constituted a "Security" and required that anyone selling security is required to disclose all of the risks of the investment necessary for the investor to make an informed decision, among other requirements.

What is Security?

Whenever someone raises money from private investors and then makes decisions on their behalf, security has been created.

Under federal and state securities laws, the sale of securities must be registered with the government as a public offering unless the sponsor or the transaction otherwise qualifies for an exemption from registration.

Can I Avoid Creation of a Security if I am Raising Private Money?

You can avoid creating security when a private lender loans money to you to purchase real estate using a promissory note and mortgage or deed of trust secured by the real estate. As long as investor funds have not been "pooled" or the record has not been "fractionalized" by combining investor funds to make up the total loan amount, this may qualify as an exempt transaction.

What if the Sponsor is Only Raising Money from Family and Friends?

It doesn't matter who the investors are, and if the sponsor is making decisions on their behalf, it's still security. However, there is an exemption from registration known as a "Private Placement" exemption that allows a sponsor to raise money from people he or she knows without registering the offering. Private Placement exemption includes the following:

– The sponsor must not engage in general solicitation or advertising of the opportunity. The sponsor must have a substantive, pre-existing relationship with any investor to whom he or she offers the securities. This is what distinguishes a Private Placement exemption from a public offering, in which general solicitation is allowed.

– The sponsor must qualify prospective investors as "accredited" or "sophisticated" based on their income, net worth, financial or investment experience, or assistance of their professional financial advisers, before their funds (i.e., "Subscription") can be accepted.

– The sponsor must disclose all foreseeable risks of the investment and may not guarantee returns. This is typically done in a Private Placement Memorandum using a format prescribed by the SEC.

– The sponsor must promptly return all money to investors if the minimum investment amount has not been raised in the time frame specified in the offering documents or if the objectives of the investment are not realized (i.e., the property is not purchased, or the company is not opened, etc.).

– A notice of the sale of securities must be filed with the SEC (Form D) and any states in which securities have been sold. The opinions (and applicable fees) must generally be presented within 15 days of the first sale of securities.

To Whom Does a Private Placement Exemption Apply?

The sponsor may be called a syndicator, promoter, manager, general partner, etc. However, regardless of title, the exemption generally applies to the issuer, i.e., the person, group or company that is selling (promoting) the securities.

What is the Usual Source of Investment Funds for a Private Placement Offering?

Investors can invest their savings or retirement funds in Private Placement offerings. The account owner can direct the custodian to release his or her retirement funds to purchase private placement interests, interests in a limited liability company or limited partnership, etc.

What If The Sponsor Doesn't Comply With Securities Laws?

Failure of the sponsor to comply with the Private Placement exemption rules may subject the investment to unnecessary legal exposure, which could impact the viability of the investment. The sponsor could be subject to substantial civil and criminal penalties for the sale of unlicensed securities. Regulatory agencies or other creditors could force liquidation at a disadvantageous time, or the sponsor could spend investor funds defending charges or paying fines.

Furthermore, a sponsor who neglects to comply with

the law may be less likely to comply with the provisions contained in the offering documents or may not understand his or her fiduciary obligations to the investors.

A syndicator who fails to follow securities laws puts the entire investment at risk.

If you are an investor contemplating investing your private funds or self-directed IRA funds, conduct your due diligence and ask questions of the sponsor. This is to determine whether the sponsor is following the rules of any applicable exemption. Also, if he has hired a securities attorney to assist with the preparation of the offering documents and compliance with the myriad securities laws."

EXAMPLES OF USING PRIVATE MONEY FOR INVESTING IN REAL ESTATE

1. When Cash is needed to acquire bargain deals or distressed properties

Private money lenders can provide cold, hard cash. When investors have access to private money, they can make offers; they usually wouldn't be able to make. This upside is significant, as nothing has the power to entice a distressed seller more than a cash offer.

Cash offers have a higher chance of being accepted, as the majority of distressed sellers do not want to deal with the burden of a bank. Along with extended closing times, the uncertainty of a conventional mortgage is another reason why sellers prefer cash offers over other financing options. The power of cash offers can also help to fuel more deals for investors.

2. When Immediate Financing is needed

It is one thing to find a real estate deal, but it is another thing entirely to fund the transaction. If you do not have the money to do the latter, you are wasting your time. In most cases, investors looking to clinch lucrative deals in real estate will need working capital to close the deal immediately. Investors looking to have the advantage of speed and efficiency when making a deal should seek private money lenders. By doing this, they can quickly secure time-sensitive deals and capitalize on opportunities that otherwise wouldn't have been available.

A private money lender will demand a cost that will be more than a traditional bank will charge. However, the benefit of a real estate investor is in the form of volume and efficiency. The opportunity to close on more deals in a shorter period is an invaluable asset for an investor.

3. When you have below-average credit scores

Private money lending affords an investor with low credit scores the opportunity to borrow money without the restrictions of traditional credit guidelines and requirements. Banks and credit unions are generally less willing to work with investors that have subpar credit or can't provide proof of a steady income. However, with a private money lender, investors can sit down and discuss their options, including negotiating the amount and terms that make sense for them.

However, this advantage comes at a cost. The use of a private money lender will entail a higher rate than other loans.

A successful real estate investor must be adept at securing capital. Such investors not only have the resources, but access to obtain working capital when needed. To make a lasting mark in real estate, investors must consider the use of a private money lender, as it can take their real estate business to the next level.

It is also important to note that not every private money lender is the same, and every lender will have their own set of rules when it comes to lending money. The critical factors to look out for before engaging a private money lender was discussed earlier.

RISKS AND DRAWBACKS OF USING PRIVATE MONEY

Although private money is a smart way to invest in real estate without using your cash, it's not a perfect solution. We have been discussing the pros of using private money, but by now, you should be aware that real estate investment is riddled with risks, and this aspect of it is not risk-free. The following paragraphs will highlight the dangers of using private money, so you'll get the full picture and decide if this is an avenue you want to pursue:

1. Legal issues

As you might have glimpsed from the chapter where the legality of private money was discussed, the validity of raising money is not easy to understand, and it differs mainly depending on location. Because of this, it is best to use a lawyer, and as we all know, lawyers are not cheap. However, hiring a lawyer to set up your business correctly at the start is much better than not doing a deal at all or sitting in a federal jail cell for doing it incorrectly.

2. Networking Required

If you have the inkling that networking is easy or quick based on how simple it sounded in our discussions, I am afraid you are lost in an illusion. It might seem harsh, but it is what it is. As with everything that has the potential to yield great results, networking does not come easy. It is a lifestyle, and if you don't like that lifestyle, you may find the process of raising private money cumbersome and confusing.

3. Higher Interest Rates

Although the rates you and your private lender agree on may not be as high as those you'd pay with a hard money lender, chances are the prices will be significantly higher than you'd see with a conventional bank. Typical private money interest rates are between 6% and 12%, depending on term length and other circumstances.

4. Personalities Are Involved

When borrowing from a bank, you are typically dealing with a system that has no emotion involved. However, borrowing from real people always consists of the potential for drama, excitement, and problems. What if your lender suddenly needs his money back? What if they get into legal trouble? These scenarios are further evidence that you need robust written legal paperwork with any lending arrangement.

SHOULD YOU USE PRIVATE MONEY?

Private money is not for everyone, but if it's an avenue you want to pursue, it can be a terrific way to raise enough capital to scale your business to new heights. Be sure you understand the risks involved and take the necessary steps upfront, so you don't get into trouble at the end.

Finally, raising private money is about having great deals, building relationships, and ultimately delivering on the promises you've made. If you can do those three things, you'll have a successful future as private money–funded real estate investor.

LEASE OPTIONS

When it comes to investing in real estate, there are just two options: you either buy and hold, or you buy and sell a property. Every investor wants to make a profit off every venture, and so, they have to play the market quite well. In the stock market, for instance, you have to be exceptional to know when to buy and sell or when to hold your stock. You can make a profit either way, but you can rarely do that at the same time. This is not always the case with real estate.

For residential real estate investors, they are in a unique position to get the best of both worlds- make a profit from buying and selling as well as buying and holding property. You may be wondering how this could be possible, and the answer is quite simple: Lease options.

WHAT IS LEASE OPTION?

A lease option is an agreement that stipulates that the renter buys the home at the end of the lease period or they would forfeit it. It also specifies that the owner cannot offer the property for sale to another person within that period. It is also known as a lease with the option to purchase and first became popular in the early 1980s as a financial instrument; it

BOB LEE

was initially used as a means to bypass alienation causes in mortgages, but it now has several advantages which include providing people who have no money with the opportunity to invest in real estate.

A lease option is better than a standard lease in the sense that it gives a potential buyer more flexibility and gives them enough time to be able to improve their credit score. Before reaching an agreement, the buyer (also known as the renter) and the owner of the home are expected to set a price on the home based on the current market value of the house. This means that you will be buying a home in the future at its worth today, and that sounds like a sweet deal. Usually, the renter is expected to pay a fee as a form of down payment, which is generally about 1% of the sale price of the home.

Generally, the terms of a lease option are negotiable, and you will be presented with two options: to pay a purchase price at the beginning of the agreement or pay the market value when the lease is due. Most people go for the former because it is expected that the amount of real estate increases with time. Besides, the duration of the lease will have to be agreed on, and it is usually between one to three years. There will also be a predetermined rental amount that the buyer will pay to the owner throughout the agreed lease period. The good thing is that all of the terms are negotiable and so, you should ensure you have all the appropriate legal advice you need before signing any agreement.

The lease option is a beneficial means of investing in real estate if you do not have enough money saved to make a down payment or if your credit score is not good enough to get you a mortgage. However, before making up your mind to use lease options, there are a few things that you should take into consideration.

Firstly, the rental payments; the owner of the home is allowed to charge a premium which is different from the monthly rent. This usually happens in cases where the buyer is going to buy the house at "today's price" at the end of the lease. The amount could be 10% of the usual monthly rental for homes of similar size and could be added to the current market rent. The premium is called 'rent credit' and is usually added to the down payment for the property. However, such fees are non-refundable, and you will forfeit all costs if you do not buy the property at the end of the lease period.

In some cases, the owners apply what is known as a "valuable consideration," which is a one-time cash payment that is quite similar to the premium paid for a typical financial market option. The amount is usually stipulated in the agreement and could be a token of about $100 to as high as 5% of the projected purchase price. So, when next you hear someone say they bought their home for $100, you best believe they are talking about lease options.

Secondly, you need to get familiar with the bank financing aspect of the lease option and how it could affect your position as a buyer or renter. In most cases, a bank will allow the total premium paid to be used as a down payment for buying the property. Nevertheless, in some situations, such as if the rent was charged based on the market rate, the bank might refuse to allow the premium to be used to buy the property. This is especially important if you plan on financing a mortgage for the property after the lease period. You should do your due diligence by checking with various banks to understand their policies on lease option purchases.

WHY LEASE OPTIONS?

There are different reasons why a buyer and the owner might have a lease option agreement. Regardless of the reasons, it is essential that you ensure that the benefits outweigh the risks before going into a lease option.

Why would a buyer enter into a lease option?

Considering our topic, the main reason we would explore is that the buyer does not have enough money or a good enough credit score to make an outright purchase. With a lease option, the buyer will be able to improve their credit score by being consistent with their monthly rentals, and at the same time, they will be saving money to buy the property.

Additionally, if a buyer has fears that the value of a particular property will go up in the future, then they can enter into a lease option. This gives them the chance to own a property in the future at today's price. It ensures that the buyer does not lose out on a potentially good deal just because they don't have the funds right now.

A buyer can also enter into a lease option even if they can afford the property. This happens when the buyer is not ready to purchase at that time due to some reasons, but they expect to be prepared in the future. This usually happens when buyers need to sell off their current home to buy a new one or when buyers want to live in a new town before making a full commitment to purchasing a house there.

Also, in a situation where the buyer needs to get a loan, but the home does not qualify for the load because of upgrades or repairs, the buyer can rent the house first and make the needed repairs before reapplying for the loan.

A lease option is an all-round win for the buyer, primarily if the agreement is structured correctly.

This brings us to the next question.

Why would a seller enter into a lease option?

The fact is that no property owner will enter into a lease option if they had other options. This is so because the owner is more restricted by the terms of a lease option than the buyer who only loses the money they paid upfront; a seller cannot sell to someone else during the duration of the lease option, regardless of what the new guys are offering.

So, in most situations, sellers who go into lease option are those who have problems selling the property outright. This may be sellers with negative equity or those who have other reasons for not wanting to sell immediately.

Negative equity refers to a situation in which the property owners owe more on their mortgage than they will be able to sell the house. If such owners have any reason to move or relocate, the best option they have is the lease option because they won't get a quick sale by putting the property on sale below the market value.

In a situation where the homeowner wants to sell the house in a few years, the lease option ensures that the buyer pays a premium that is higher than the current market rent to the seller. In a situation where the renter decides not to buy the house, the seller still gets to keep the monthly rental and the premium, and they can put the house back on the market.

So, it could be a win for the seller also, if they play their cards right and are not in negative equity.

NO MONEY DOWN INVESTING WITH A LEASE OPTION

We have seen the possible reasons why you as a potential investor (buyer) should be interested in lease options. But, to summarize, here are the reasons again:

You do not need to have a lot of money to enter into a lease option. In most cases, you only need to have the "valuable consideration," which could be as little as $100.

You do not need to take out a mortgage

You will be making money every month

You can have "instant equity" by buying the property if its value rises above the agreed purchase price.

If the value of the property falls, you can choose not to buy the property at no extra cost other than the nonrefundable monthly rentals.

How does this work for someone with no money? We will illustrate with an example:

Assume Mr. Jones has a lease option with these terms:

- The property is currently worth $90,000, and he has the option of buying it for $100,000

- The option period is five years
- He pays the owner $1 to get the opportunity
- He spends the owner $300 per month, which covers their mortgage payment
- He rents out the property I rent the property out for $600 per month and spends about $100 per month on expenses like maintenance and repairs. This means he makes $200 profit every month.

In five years, there are three possible scenarios:

- The property is now worth $110,000. He buys the property for the agreed price of $100,000 after taking out a mortgage. He just got a $10,000 discount and made $12,000 in rent while at it.
- The value of the property hasn't changed. He decides not to buy it at $100,000 but instead gives the property back to the owner. He has made $12,000 in profit from rent.
- He could decide to sell the lease option to someone who wants to buy the property. If he sells at $10,000, they would also pay $100,000 to the owner of the property. He would have $12,000 from rent and $10,000 from the sale, a total of $22,000.

Whatever the scenario, Mr. Jones wins. Now, try to make these projections using larger values depending on the kind of property you have your eyes on. The possible profit is astounding, yes?

Well, that's what makes lease options so great. You win, anyway, even when you do not have any money to invest with.

There is, therefore, no gainsaying that you will need to find a property owner who will be interested in a lease option. The first thing to bear in mind is that lease options are more accessible with owners who have negative equity and also needs to move or relocate. Their reasons could include divorce, relocating, expansion of the family, and so on. Then you need to do your research and find the people who fall into that category. You may use the internet to locate them by running Ads on facebook or Google targeting people who could be a match to your already predetermined demographics; you could also search for some localities that you suspect might have people with negative equity, you may also use agents to locate people who just want to enter into a lease option even if they don't have negative equity, and finally, you may check for properties that are being advertised for sale at prices that are higher than their current market worth, mainly if they were sold at high prices in the past.

It is not a walk in the park if you have to search for people who fit the bill by yourself, but at the end of the day, as an investor, anything that is worth doing is worth doing well.

RISK AND DRAWBACKS OF THE LEASE OPTION

It is important to note that it is always better to own a property completely rather than employing some of these strategies we have explored. However, there is no perfect strategy when it comes to real estate investments, and lease option is not an exception.

The risks could arise from the owner of the property, and it could also arise from the tenant or buyer. It is vital to bear in mind that the original owner would have probably not agreed to the lease terms if they were in a high financial position in the first place. So, you're relying on them to cooperate with you for the duration of your agreement. This exposes you to a lot of risks, which include:

Nonrefundable Fees. In a situation where you are not allowed to exercise your lease option, you will most likely incur huge losses. There's the non-refundable option fee, the payment for repairs and the higher lease payment. Everything would have been done in vain.

Expensive legal action. This could happen in a situation where the owner refuses to allow you to exercise the option. You may end up spending more money than needed in legal fees.

Owner "flaking out." This happens when the owner does not pay the mortgage, and the lender comes to repossess the property. This is made even worse when you have been making your agreed monthly payments. The property will be foreclosed on, and the buyer will lose their position, especially during housing downturns.

Expensive repair and maintenance work. In a situation where you have to do a lot of repairs on the property, so much so that you end up spending your profit and may start incurring losses if you do not take extra care.

Breach of lease. This could be due to several reasons including having incorrect insurance, lack of proper legal advice, and so on. If your contract was created without the guidance of an attorney, or if you only had a gentleman's agreement, it may not hold up in court if you ever need to take legal action. For instance, if the terms are not spelled out in your contract, the owner may back out and claim there was no legal agreement. And, you would be left with nothing from the deal.

The risk of the property getting devalued. In most cases, you would expect that the property will appreciate over time. However, depending on several factors that drive the market cycle, the property may be worth way less at the expiration of the contract. You may be unable to renegotiate the agreed purchase price and would have to bear the brunt of the difference.

You should also always remember that regardless of the amount that you pay or have paid to the seller, you still do not own the house until the seller agrees to hand over full control at the expiration of the lease. So, you may have to put up with feeling like a tenant in a house that you are paying a premium for. Additionally, you may lose out on a property you planned to purchase if, at the end of the period, you are not able to boost your credit ratings enough or save up for the full payment.

Most of the risks that you face as a buyer in lease options can be prevented by carrying out the necessary research and doing your due diligence on the property as well as the prospective seller.

The worst risks or disadvantages of a lease option apply to the seller who has to bear the brunt of the effects of uncertainty. The lease option contracts usually last for years, and if at the end of the period, the buyer decides not to buy the property, then the seller must go through the cycle again, expending more money, time and energy back. In a situation where the property depreciates, and the buyer decides not to buy, then the seller/owner will have to sell the same property for an amount that is lower than the original value as at the time the lease was agreed on. If there were no lease, the seller would have probably sold the property long before the value dropped.

LEASE OPTION WRAP-UP

A lease option agreement is a real estate investment strategy that provides more benefit to the buyer than it does to the seller. Usually, a lease to own gives more freedom and power to the buyer to do as they would like without exposing them to high risks. Generally, no seller would go into a lease option agreement unless they have no other choice or option of selling their property; the average seller would rather sell the property outright than go into a lease option that exposes them to so many risks.

To fully protect your position as a buyer, you should ensure that the terms of your lease agreement are favorable and you should employ the services of an attorney. Here are some details to pay attention to in any lease option agreement:

Utilities. The contract should state the existing utilities in the property and should also specify who would pay for any additional services included in the house.

Maintenance and repairs. You would be doing yourself a great disservice if you spend a lot of money to fix up a property, only to find out that the money spent is non-refundable and will not be deducted from your monthly premium or the final sum to be paid to buy the property.

Taxes and insurance:

The agreement should specify the full details of coverage and should also make it mandatory for the seller to make all necessary payments. You should also discuss with your attorney on the best means to ensure that you are entirely indemnified in case of any damages or costs that may arise while the lease is active.

Several occupants. These are some minor terms that may result in a breach of a lease agreement. So, ensure that you spell it out clearly to avoid losing out on your lease for avoidable reasons.

Renovations. If there is any need to renovate, you and the seller should reach an agreement on who will pay for it and how the payment should be made. Do not leave it to a handshake agreement; ensure it is put in writing.

Primary residence or investment. This is also a vital part of the lease option agreement. You should make sure the purpose for which the property is to be used is spelled out in the transaction.

In conclusion, there is no gainsaying that lease options are one of the best real estate investment strategies for you if you do not have enough money to make a down payment on a property. So, as a potential buyer, if you do lay your hands on a lease option agreement, ensure to milk it for all of its benefits. However, always remember the legal aspect that could make or mar the entire process for you.

SELLER FINANCING

This is another strategy that could be used when one is interested in having investments, but one does not have sufficient capital to start with. In straightforward terms, seller financing is a loan provided by the seller of a business or a property to the buyer. In real estate, it involves the seller or owner handling the mortgage processes instead of a bank or financial institution. This means that the buyer would sign a mortgage with the owner of the property instead of signing with a traditional bank. Seller financing is also known as owner financing and a purchase-money lease.

A purchase-money mortgage is a mortgage that the seller of a home issue to the borrower or buyer as part of the purchase transaction. It is usually applied in situations where the buyer is unable to get a mortgage through the regular channels, generally due to a bad credit score. It is used where the buyer agrees to assume the seller's mortgage and the difference between the price of the property when putting on sale and the assumed lease is made up with seller financing. So, the buyer provides down payment, and a financial instrument is issued, which is recorded in public records to offer the ultimate protection to both parties involved in the transaction.

What is Seller Financing?

In a seller-financed transaction, the seller doubles as the lender. However, the seller doesn't hand over money to a buyer in the form of a loan; instead, the buyer is allowed to make payments over an agreed period. It can even be applied to first-time renters, and in a short time, you can become the owner of the property. The most appealing thing about seller financing to the owner is that they would be relieved of the expenses of property tax, maintenance, and homeowners insurance because they are usually paid by the buyer in a deal like this.

Seller financing deals are usually short-termed and will involve the buyer signing a promissory note that they will give to the seller; the letter will contain details of the agreed interest rate, payment plan and consequences of defaulting on a payment. Usually, the loan is amortized over 30 years but with a balloon payment that is due in a few years because it is expected that the buyer's credit should have improved and they should be able to pay up. Nobody wants to have their property "locked down" for thirty years while waiting for a buyer to pay up the loan.

In most cases, seller financing involves the buyer making a balloon payment many years after the sale has been completed. A balloon payment is a large payment that is made at the end of some loans such as a commercial loan or a mortgage. It is usually issued for a short term with the final payment being more significant than the other installments.

Types of Seller Financing

Here are some of the most common types of seller financing.

- Junior Mortgage. The average lender will not finance more than 80% of the value of a home, thereby leaving the buyer with 20% of the payment to source for. In this case, the seller can extend some credit to the buyer to make up the 20% required. The seller is said to carry the "junior" or second mortgage for the difference in the purchase price and any down payment made. Thus, the seller will get the proceeds from the first mortgage from the buyer's primary financier. However, in the case of a foreclosure or if the buyer defaults on payments, the seller accepts a lower priority; this means that they will only get paid after the first mortgage has been settled and if there are enough proceeds left over from the sales.

- All-Inclusive Mortgage. In this case, the seller bears the promissory note and mortgage for the total cost of the property, minus the down payment.
- Land Contract. The buyer is given an "equitable" title, which means temporary shared ownership. The buyer will not get the deed or land contracts until they make the final payment.
- Assumable Mortgage. This option makes it possible for the buyer to take over the sellers' existing mortgage. This is usually done with the approval of the bank.
- Lease options. This involves the seller agreeing to lease the property to the buyer for an agreed period after the payment of a fee. The details have been discussed in the previous section.

The popularity of seller financing depends on several market conditions, but most notably, the state of the credit market. Usually, seller financing is more favorable when banks are being more careful about the risks they are willing to take on. This means that when banks are not willing to lend money to anybody but people with the best credit scores, seller financing comes to the rescue and makes it possible for people to buy a property or sell them, as the case may be. Conversely, when the banks are "happy" and willing to lend out money with less stringent requirements, seller financing loses its appeal.

THE PROBLEM WITH SELLER FINANCING

Seller financing could be the answer to your prayers about investing in real estate with no money; however, there are problems that accompany this particular investment strategy. These problems arise when the deal is not structured correctly with the help of an experienced real estate attorney. The cost of such issues could be very significant for both the buyer and the seller.

For a buyer, problems could arise if there are existing loans on the property being sold and the seller does not own the property entirely and so, the current mortgage will have to be transferred to them. This means that the buyer will be making a payment on the loan, just like the owner was doing. In some cases, the loan may be unassumable, which means that the transfer to a new owner could trigger a due on sales clause in the mortgage. This makes it impossible for the original lender to accept payments from the new buyer and so, they could lose the house in foreclosure, especially if they cannot get a new loan.

For a seller, the most common problem arises when the seller's loan comes due for payment. In several instances, the buyer claims that there were undisclosed problems with the property in a bid to further drive down the price of the property. Also, in a situation where the buyer can only qualify for a certain amount of loan, and the loan is held in the first position, the seller may give the buyer an additional credit to make up the difference. However, this loan will be held in the second position, which means that unless the first mortgage is paid off, the seller may not get their own money back.

Due to the myriad of problems that may arise, sellers and buyers are advised to make sure that their promissory notes contain all the details required for the deal to go through.

Why should you buy using seller financing?

One of the best features of seller financing is the fact that it cuts out the middleman (usually banks and mortgage lenders) involved in the sale of any property.

Generally, the buyers who are interested in seller financing are those who have difficulties with getting a loan from the bank or financial institutions. The most popular reason is usually a case of bad credit which seller financing thankfully helps you to bypass. Seller financing allows the buyer have some measure of flexibility with the down payment; so, if the seller wants a down payment that is higher than what the buyer has, the buyer can be allowed to make the payment of lump sums at periodic intervals to make up the down payment.

Usually, to get a bank mortgage, you would have to go through a rigorous process of appraisal and vetting, which generally takes up a lot of time and may not end the way you would like. Seller financing, on the other hand, may skip the appraisal process, and it is also much faster, and you could have a deal within a week. The process is usually less stringent and is more flexible on many points, including loan interest rates; interest rates may be adjusted based on market factors, or it could be kept constant throughout the loan.

Another beautiful thing about this investment strategy is that it offers the option of tailored financing, which means that the buyers and sellers can choose the loan repayment option that works best for them. They could opt for any of interest-only, less-than-interest, fixed-rate amortization, or a balloon payment, or they could go for a combination of the options depending on state laws.

Also, seller financing usually involves few or no closing costs, unlike a bank mortgage. The term 'closing costs' refers to any expense that is more than the price of the property, and it is usually incurred by both the seller and the buyer in any real estate transaction. Such costs may include appraisal fees, discount points, taxes, title insurance, credit report charges, loan origination fees, survey, and title searches. Usually, the actual value of the closing costs depends on the value of the property being transferred and where the property is being sold. And, it may be paid by either the buyer or the seller. The closing costs must be agreed on before the deal is completed. For seller financing, all of these costs are excluded.

If you are in a hurry to get a deal closed with as little hassles as possible, then the seller financing option is just perfect for you. Since the sellers and buyers are not waiting for a mediator to process the deal, they can close faster and transfer possession in record time.

WHY SHOULD YOU SELL USING SELLER FINANCING?

The most attractive feature of seller financing for the sellers is that it makes it possible to get your property sold quickly. If you're a seller who is having problems with getting your home sold, seller financing can make your home stand out, thus making you close the deal faster. You will be able to attract a different set of buyers and will turn your hitherto "difficult to sell" situation around.

Also, you may be able to avoid the burden of extra repairs which may be expensive because you may be able to sell the house as it is. This is vastly different from what is obtainable with traditional financial institutions that require the seller to carry out several repairs before they can close a deal on the property.

With seller financing, you may be able to get better interest rates when compared with other investments. This includes other low-risk investments or a money market account. Also, the seller might pay lesser taxes because payments are received on an installment basis. They would only have to report the income received per year, effectively reducing their payable fee.

Also, the payments made by a buyer every month (or at the agreed period) will serve as a new form of cash flow for the seller. This will help increase their spendable income and even make them more comfortable.

Another critical reason why sellers consider seller-financing is because it puts them in a situation to demand a higher price for their property. And, this makes sense because the seller is offering the financing for the property, anyway and the buyer may have no option but to pay a higher price at the end of the day.

In a situation where the buyer defaults on their payment without notice, the seller will get the house back, and they get to keep any money that had been paid, including the down payment. So, technically, it is a win-win situation for the seller. Also, the seller can sell the promissory note at a discount, thereby making a lump sum in a single deal.

Even though it seems straightforward, the procedures involved in seller financing could be sophisticated and prospective buyers, and sellers should endeavor to get legal advice from real estate lawyers before committing to any deals. This will ensure that all interested parties are protected regardless of the outcome of the agreement.

Example of a seller-financed deal

Let's say you were able to find a seller who owns their home free and clear with no mortgage and the property is pegged at $200,000. Let's say you don't have the money, meaning you would have to go to the bank and borrow the $200,000 or whatever fraction of it that you can get based on your credit score. But, what if you are unable to borrow from the bank or any lending house because you have poor credit, you are self-employed, and you do not have a valid source of income, or you have maxed out your credit?

With seller financing, you could offer a deal to the seller; agree to buy the house for $200,000 but instead of buying the property outright, you would make a principal down payment, say $20,000 and then the seller will carry the balance of $180,000 which will be written in a promissory note and secured by a first mortgage. You would also propose making monthly payments, which will include the principal, about a 7% interest rate and will be calculated for the usual 30 years.

However, no seller will be willing to tie down their homes for 30 years. So, you can expect to make a balloon payment after a few years. The balloon payment could come after 15 years, and it is usually a lump sum, which, when paid, makes you the owner of the property.

For the down payment, you should expect the seller to ask for 5%-25% of the asking price as a down payment.

The agreement would be something like this:

Asking Price	**$200,000**
Down payment	$20,000
Financed Amount	$180,000
Interest Rate	7%
Amortization	30-year repayment plan
Balloon	At 15 years
Monthly Payment (principal and interest)	$1,197.54
Balance Due at Time of Balloon	$147,570
Total of all Payments Made to Seller (Down payment +monthly payment for 15 years+ balloon payment)	$383,127

When it is time to make the balloon payment, you can either pay the full sum of $147,570 from your savings or borrow the money to pay off the seller. If you end up borrowing, then you have to get a new loan payment yet again.

THREE WAYS TO FIND SELLER-FINANCED DEALS

There will always be people who are willing to sell the property to you; however, not all of them will be willing to enter into a seller-financed deal. So, it is essential that you know how to find these sellers and get yourself a sweet deal.

Talk to a real estate agent. If you find a home that you want to buy, your agent can approach the owner on your behalf to find out if they are interested in selling and would not mind seller financing

Check the internet for multiple listing service sites for properties on sale that comes with owner financing. You can also check for homes with a lease option; usually, these sellers are more open to exploring seller financing options because they want to move house fast.

Find "burned-out" landlords. This means landlords and owners who are fed up with their current tenants and other details of rental ownership and want to sell off their property. Some sellers who fit the profile will fall into one or more of these categories:

Owners who don't live on the farm and are never around. You can find them via online sources like

CRSdata.com, realquest.com or listsource.com among others

Landlords who are battling with eviction court cases. They are already at the apex of the frustration curve with their tenants and would not mind selling

Vacant houses or houses that have been on the market for a long time are usually primed for seller financing, and you will be offering the owners a great relief.

In addition to all of these tips, the importance of networking cannot be overemphasized; when you participate in real estate meetups and events, you will meet investors who want to sell a property, and you can pitch your idea to them. With the proper motivation and agreed terms, you will have a seller-financed deal in no time and will be well on your way to becoming a homeowner.

The importance of contracts to the success of real estate investing cannot be overemphasized. The terms of the contract or agreement are essential, and these are a few of them:

-   Price. There is usually a relationship between the price of a property and the terms of the sale. You have to take care to ensure that you do not end up paying more than the property is worth. The reason why you want the property will also determine just how much you are willing to pay for it. So, you should carry out an analysis of your real estate goals ahead of time and decide what would be a fair price for you to pay on the property. If the property is situated in a prime location, then you could pay higher for it; however, if it is in a depressed area, or you are not planning to hold the house for a long time, you should try to push the price as low as possible.

- Down payment: The percentage that you would pay as down payment depends on the seller and what you both agree on. Most sellers would usually propose down fee of 5% to 25% of the purchase price, but they might be willing to go lower. So, you should not hesitate to ask for lesser percentages. In some cases, you could also use other property as down payment such as trucks, land, or even a promissory note. You are allowed to be as creative as possible with your down payment options. Also, if the property would require lots of repairs, you should find a way to deduct the repair costs from your down payment.

- Interest Rate Amount. Ensure you negotiate an interest rate that is as low as possible so that you do not end up paying more than you should. You may even be able to go as little as 4% depending on your negotiation skills and other factors taken into consideration.

- The payment amount and start date. If your payment is amortized, which means it would include the interest and the principal, to be paid at set intervals. It is essential that you negotiate a payment plan that would favor you in every way.

- Maturity Date. This is the date when it is expected that you must have made all the payments and can now get the deeds to the house. However, with balloon payments, you would likely make the lump sum payment by this time. Ensure that the time set is convenient and feasible on every front. Otherwise, you may lose the house and all your debts with it.

Other terms that should be clearly explained in your contract include the on sale clause, the substitution of security, stepped-up and accruing interest, as well as legal fees. You need to be specific as to who pays for what and when.

RISKS AND DRAWBACKS OF SELLER FINANCING

The major drawback of seller financing for buyers is that they usually end up paying a higher interest than they would have paid if they had gotten a mortgage from a bank or a financial institution. When factored in and added to all the other payments, the option will cost more money in the long run. But then, it offers the flexibility that banks don't.

Also, sellers face the risk of the buyers defaulting on their payment. This could result in a significant loss for the seller, and since they do not have employees to help them chase down the buyer and get their money back, they have to put up with the stress by themselves. In the process of trying to get the buyer to make a payment, they will also incur legal charges which the buyer might be ordered to pay by a court. However, if the buyer files for bankruptcy, then the seller cannot get their money back until the house is sold.

The "balloon payment" could also be a problem in the long run, especially if the buyer is unable to meet up with the required payment. So, the buyer has to ensure that they continuously work on their credit while saving up or making more money for the balloon payment.

In a situation where the buyer defaults and the seller now has to bear some more costs and foreclose on the property, the seller would have to pay the repair costs. This is especially true if the buyer mismanaged the property and caused a lot of damage in the process.

Also, there could be problems with the tax calculations because of the flexibility of the entire process; even if you can negotiate 0% interest rate as a buyer, the seller will still have to file profit for taxes, and it could be quite complicated if not handled properly.

To avoid some of these pitfalls, here are some tips for you:

Always work with a real estate attorney in addition to your real estate agent. They are usually more experienced in writing sales contracts and will guide you better on how to craft your promissory note. This applies to both sellers and buyers.

Even though the process is supposed to be less stringent than traditional lending, it is best that sellers run a credit check on their prospective buyers before sealing a deal. You'll be able to avoid a situation where someone suddenly decides to stop making payments, and you're left stranded.

Always get professional guidance when calculating your taxes, as well as the effect that a seller-financed deal will have on it.

As a buyer turned investor with bad credit, you should focus on raising your credit score, so you can refinance before the balloon payment is due.

PARTNERSHIPS IN REAL ESTATE INVESTMENT

This is another strategy that you can use when getting into real estate investment, and you do not have the capital to start with. When seeking advice or doing your research, you must have been told to get into a real estate partnership. The first question you would ask yourself is whether it is a good idea, and why would anyone want to go into business with you when you do not have any money of yours to invest? Well, there is more to companies than meets the eyes.

Real Estate Investment partnerships could be advantageous in the sense that they help create a delicate balance of all the advantages that you and your partner will be bringing to the table. In the same vein, if not adequately managed, real estate investment partnerships could turn out to be very disastrous indeed.

Why should you go into a real estate investment partnership?

Firstly, this is the only form of real estate investment in which all the parties involved are committed to seeing it work because they all "have some skin in the game" and so it isn't tilted to one side more than the other. Besides, it helps to bring different resources together to improve the profitability of the venture. It is important to note that resources include financial, workforce, knowledge, skills, and network, among others. It is not uncommon to find a situation in which one of the partners has the necessary background knowledge about real estate investment, but they do not have the financial resources with which to make it work. In this situation, the partner should be someone who has the money and who will allow the other partner to make their investment decisions. Another example is when someone has a bad credit score, but they always find great deals; the partner will be someone with good credit who can qualify for loans when needed.

Partnerships also make it possible to share the risks of the business. There is no gainsaying that real estate investment is prone to risks and could be significantly affected by market conditions, so, a partnership will ensure that the risk is spread out among the partners. It is important to note that the risk is usually shared based on their shares in the business, so someone with higher percentages bears more risk. This is also advantageous because everyone will be committed to the growth of the market.

It could also improve the efficiency of the work process by sharing tasks or division of labor. Real estate investment usually involves a lot of steps that could be time-consuming; for instance, property management, financial records, tenancy agreements, and management, etc. It could be quite challenging for one person to manage it all, but with partnerships, these tasks can be shared among the partners so that each person is responsible for something specific.

Real Estate investment partnership will also help with improved accountability among the partners. They can all be held accountable for their actions per time and will also have to ensure they always act in the best interest of the company. On the same note, they would be able to prevent wrong decision by double-checking every deal they have to make.

As you probably know already, networking is the soul of real estate investment business, and as such, you should endeavor to build a profitable network as much as possible. With partnerships, you are guaranteed an expanded network of useful connections, and thereby, you can grow your business opportunities.

Why you may not want to join a real estate investment partnership

It is essential that you understand that having a partner does not automatically mean you will start making more money; instead, you will be sharing your profit even if you are making as much money as you were making before when you were alone. Depending on the kind of partnership you entered into, you may be sharing the profit 50/50 or 30/70, which means you could be getting 70% or 30% of the profit. If you have more partners, then you might even make less. Therefore, you have to be prepared for that and make sure you are okay with anything you earn after the profit is shared. Otherwise, you may be better off being on your own.

Dealing with taxes in a real estate investment partnership is a different kettle of fish; it is more complicated because instead of handling filing for taxes alone, it now has to be shared among all the partners. If you were alone, you would be 100% responsible for filing, but soon that other people are involved, filing becomes more complicated and if not properly managed can result in problems for the business.

Another factor to consider is the matter of control and final decision making on issues that concern the business. As a sole investor, you have full control over what you would like to do with your property. However, in a partnership, you cannot call the shots without the other members agreeing to it; this can result in disagreements which if not properly managed, can cause the business to fold up. Sometimes, it would not even matter if you have the best ideas for your business to grow if the partners do not approve of it, then nothing gets done about it.

Overall, a real estate partnership can be a huge success, or it can be a nightmare. The challenge is in finding the right investment partner who is ready to be 100% committed to the business. If you do find one, you may end up making multiples of your profit as a sole investor. As usual, you may have to rely on your network to find the person that fits into your goal for your business.

When considering investing in real estate with a partner, here are some tips to help you make the best choice.

Find out what your prospective partner is bringing to the business and make sure they are verifiable. Do they have the financial capacity to put their money where their mouth is? Do they have the necessary skills and knowledge base that would be an immense addition to your business?

If you don't trust them as people, then you have no business getting into a partnership with them. You need trust to be able to see any deal through to completion.

You must all agree on the objectives of your business and how you intend to achieve them.

Ask for proof of success; usually, the 5-deal rule of thumb will apply here. It means that your prospective client should be able to give you evidence of 5 completed deals.

Make sure you spell out the exit strategies for your business so that if any partner wants to leave at any time, the company does not have to fold up.

Try as much as possible to have well-defined roles and responsibilities from the very beginning. It would help you avoid the blame game and will make sure your work runs more effectively

OWNER-OCCUPIED INVESTMENT PROPERTIES

AS the name, suggests, means that the property owner also lives in the same property and has the title deed to the property. For instance, when you buy a property as an investor, and you choose to live in one of the units while you rent the other groups out, the property is called "owner-occupied." It is essential, however, to note that you must have lived on the farm for at least two consecutive years for it to be called an owner-occupied home.

What are the advantages of having owner-occupied investment properties?

For first time or beginner real estate investors, this is a great way to start building your real estate business. It is a strategy that allows you to learn how to manage a rental property on the job. It is a lot easier to manage because you will never be at a loss as to what is going on in your property. Since you live on the same farm, you will be able to make sure your tenants are taking care of the property, and it also makes it easier to collect rent. Also, your tenants are more likely to behave appropriately when they know, you are living next door.

Besides, it is a relatively inexpensive investment. To

start with, you can buy a duplex while you're living on one side of the building and then you will use the rent money from the other units to cover the mortgage payment. It means that you can live without making payments until the property is finally paid off. In most cases, you will only be required to put down 3.5% of the value, and then when you include the incoming rent from tenants, you should be able to qualify for a much larger loan.

In some cases, multi-unit owner-occupied properties are more accessible to finance than single investment properties. You can qualify for several loans with the smaller down payment, better interest rates, and more flexible requirements. As an investor, you can use the fact that you will be living on the property as a bargaining chip. With this investment strategy, you can qualify for the VA loan, FHA loan, and conventional loan, among others.

Why you may not want to buy into owner-occupied investment properties

Challenges come with owner-occupied investment, and they will either have you throwing the towel, or you could try to bounce back at every turn.

Even though there are advantages to living in the same home with your tenants, the fact remains that tenants are a handful, and they could be frustrating. Some tenants make complaints all the time, and your proximity to them means they have easy access to you at all time. You can get over this challenge by making strict rules about when and how to file complaints about the home.

You may also have a difficult time getting tenants who want to live in the same house as the landlord; most people prefer to live as far away from the landlord as possible. You can reduce the impact of this limitation by making sure your home and prices are competitive, and you have all the necessary amenities and more. There is no doubt that if you have a lot to offer, you will get potential tenants in droves.

Another challenge with this investment strategy is that there could be conflicts of interest between you and the tenants. For instance, it may be more difficult to enforce some rules if you and your tenants have close personal relationships. You will find it challenging to make unbiased business decisions and to invest calls.

So, you have to be able to set the boundaries between you and your tenants and make sure you are upfront about everything about the property. It should help prevent any conflict of interest that may arise.

Investing in owner-occupied properties is an excellent real estate investment strategy because it opens up opportunities for better financing, and it also allows you to live in the house for free. And by taking proper care of the property, you will be able to receive rent and will be better positioned to get more loans which you can now invest in other features.

HOME EqUITY LOAN

This is a second mortgage in which one intends to borrow in one lump sum and pay it back every month. The period for Home Equity Loan is typically five to fifteen years. The payment and interest rate remains the same over the life of the loan. The loan must be repaid fully on the home in which it is sold. In-Home Equity Loan, one can get a lower interest rate than what one would qualify to receive on loan without putting collateral. For HEL, the bank allows the loanee to loan money against the equity of his or her property issued with a lump sum. The interest in HEL is on a fixed rate and fixed payment

THE CREDIT SCORE ONE NEEDS TO GET HOME EqUITY LOAN

Credit Score is a numerical expression based on a level analysis of a person's credit file to represent the creditworthiness of an individual. To qualify for HEL, one must have a maximum loan to value ratio or LTO of 80 percent to 20 percent equity in the home. One must also have a documented ability to repay the loan. Essentially, a home equity loan is a mortgage. The investment in the house is used as collateral for the loan. The amount the loanee is allowed to borrow is partially based on a combined loan to value (CLTV) ratio of 80% to 90% of the worth of the home. It is a way of converting equity over a home into use by putting the house in line. In HEL a loaner is willing to borrow against the full amount of home equity. Generally, it is about 75-90 percent of available capital.

ADVANTAGES OF HOME EqUITY LOAN

1. It has lower interest rates than other loans. They also typically come with a fixed interest rate.

2. It is an easy way to get a large sum of money in a short time.

3. It is a secured loan that is secured by one's home value.

4. The loan may be tax-deductible, which means it is removed from the taxable income, hence lowering the overall tax expense liability.

5. One is paid in cash when one takes up a home equity loan.

6. The lender, as lenders have a tangible asset, they can repossess. If the borrower fails to pay the debt, the lender automatically gets possession of the house.

DISADVANTAGES OF HOME EqUITY LOAN

1. One is at risk of losing one's home to the financial institution or lender if it fails to repay the debt.

2. Never consider a home equity loan if making risky monetary decisions. If one is starting a business whose chances of success are moderate, then one should opt-out of a home equity loan.

3. Although it is an easy way to get money to pay off loans, or to get a student loan, the borrower might sink even deeper into debt if they take up a second loan to pay off the first.

4. There is a very high chance of facing bankruptcy if one takes out a home equity loan that's worth more than the net worth o the home

HOW TO FIND THE BEST HOME EqUITY, LENDER

The following are the best Home Equity Lender:

Lending Tree: Lending Tree Home Equity Loan is the overall best lender

Citizens Bank: Citizens Bank Home Equity Loan are also useful because they offer their services at a lower cost.

TD Bank: TD Bank Home Equity Loan is best for Home Equity Loan Credit

Chase: Chase Home Equity Loan is best for seniors

Wells Fargo: Wells Fargo Home Equity Loan is best for those in bad debt.

HOME EqUITY LINE OF CREDIT

Home equity line of credit or equity line of credit is a loan for a range of created for some maximum draw, preferably for a fixed amount. HELOC has a draw period during which the borrower can use the front and a repayment period which must be repaid. The draw period for the equity line of credit is between five to fifteen years, during which the loanee pays interest over the drawn amount. Repayment of the drawn amount commences from ten to twenty years where the loanee pays principle equal to the balance at the end of the draw period divided by the number of months in the repayment period.

INTEREST ON HOME EqUITY LINE OF CREDIT

Because the balance of a HELOC is likely to change day by day depending on draws and repayment interest on HELOC is calculated daily. The interest in HELOC in the range of 6%.

ADVANTAGES OF HOME EqUITY LINE OF CREDIT

- It is suitable for constant needs, such as paying off a credit card, making a house improvement, paying college tuition, investing in real estate, paying for a vacation, etc. HELOC can be converted to fixed-rate loans when drawn. It is suitable for loanee who wants to get a large amount of money
- It has little or no closing cost especially when it has a good credit
- It is financially flexible. You can only pay on what you loaned
- Another advantage of HELOC is that there are no restrictions on the use of fund
- Loaners are also not charged for drawing fund from a HELOC

DISADVANTAGES OF HOME EqUITY LINE OF CREDIT

- HELOC had an interest rate risk. All HELOC are Adjustable Risk Mortgages(ARMs) and are much riskier than standard ARMs.
- If one defaults in HELOC, there is a risk of possible foreclosure, I.e., one can lose ones home
- Another chance is that the loaner has the right to cut off unused credit lined, especially in times of financial crisis.

- Using all the available credit on your HELOC may have a negative effect and affect ones credit score as it's an indicator of high risk even if one make payments on time

DOES CLOSING A HELOC AFFECT CREDIT SCORE?

Part of your credit score is determined by your credit utilization, which is how much credit you are using. Closing a HELOC decreases how much credit you have, which can affect your overall credit score. However, if you have other credit lines beside a HELOC like credit cards, then closing it should have minimal effect on your credit score. Another reason to close the line of credit if you don't need to take any more money out or if you pay off the balance is that it will close out the lien on your home that a HELOC puts in place as collateral. If you want to sell your home and purchase another, then you would first need to close out the HELOC.

DIFFERENCE BETWEEN HOME EqUITY LOAN AND HOME EqUITY LINE OF CREDIT

- DELIVERY OF FUNDS

HEL -One lump sum

HOLEC - One is approved for an amount that can be withdrawn as needed during a period established by the lender

- CATEGORIES OF INTEREST RATE

HEL-ones monthly payment and rate remains the same month-to-month, though, the variable interest rate may change if the rate index changes.

HELOC- fixed rates are more, and there may be a fee associated with the rate conversion

- LENGTH OF REPAYMENT

HEL- 5 to 30 years, at the loaner's discretion

HELOC- 10 to 30 years, at d loaner's discretion.

- CLOSING COST FEE

HEL- Depends on the lender, but can include application, origination, and appraisal fees, and also closing costs.

HELOC- one does not pay these fees.

- ANNUAL PAYMENT

HEL- No annual fees

HELOC- have yearly fees

- TAX

HEL- The interest paid is tax-deductible if the money borrowed is used for home renovations.

HELOC- The interest paid is tax-deductible if the money borrowed is used for home renovations.

- PREPAYMENT

HEL- It depends on the loaner

HELOC-it depends on the loaner as well

ALTERNATIVE TO HOME EqUITY LOAN

A personal loan is typically an unsecured loan that offers you access to cash that can be used towards debt consolidation, home improvements, or usually whatever else one needs money for. Personal loans are generally provided with fixed interest rates that are lower than other financing options, allowing for a straightforward repayment process.

CREDIT CARD

Credit cards offer a line of credit that is similar to a HELOC. While this makes borrowing for any purpose easy, it is also incredibly expensive. Average credit card interest rates can vary be between 20% and 30%. They are also typically about twice as high as personal loan interest rates.

Credit cards can be useful if one needs a large amount of money fast, but it's best to plan to pay it off within a few months.

PROPERTУ VALUATION

Value is the present worth of future benefit arising from the ownership of the property. The advantage of real estate is realized in the future. So in determining the value of a feature on must take cognizance of economic and social trends, governmental controls, and environmental conditions.

Land valuation is the process of developing an opinion of value, for real property (usually market value). Real estate transactions often require appraisals because they occur infrequently and every feature is unique (especially their condition, a key factor in valuation), unlike corporate stocks, which are traded daily and are identical (thus a centralized Walrasian auction like a stock exchange is unrealistic). The location also plays a crucial role in valuation. However, since property cannot change location, it is often the upgrades or improvements to the home that can change its value. Appraisal reports form the basis for mortgage loans, settling estates and divorces, taxation, and so on. Sometimes an appraisal report is used to establish a sale price for a property.

ELEMENTS OF VALUE

- DEMAND: Is the ability and willingness to obtain property. It is ownership supported with purchasing power.

- UTILITY: is the amount of satisfaction one gets from buying real property. It is the ability to satisfy future owners their taste, desires, or needs in real estate.
- SCARCITY: Is created by over demand or unavailability and inaccessibility of real property. It is the finite supply of competing properties
- TRANSFERABILITY: the property should be able to be transferred easily

WHAT CONSTITUTES MARKET VALUE?

Market value – The market value appraisal is the estimate of the cost of a particular property as of a specific date, and it helps in determining the market value of the property. The market price may not necessarily determine the amount of the property, for example, distress sale. The market price is the price at which an asset would trade in a competitive Walrasian auction setting. Market value is usually interchangeable with open market value or fair value. It can also be said to be the estimated amount for which an asset or liability should exchange on the valuation date between a willing buyer and a willing seller in an arm's length transaction, after proper marketing and where the parties had each acted knowledgeably, prudently and without compulsion.

DISTINCTION BETWEEN PRICE AND VALUE

Price is not a determiner of value. A property might be sold (price) below or above its value. There can be differences between what the property is worth (market value) and what it cost to buy it (price). A price paid might not represent that property's market value. Sometimes, special considerations may have been present, such as a special relationship between the buyer and the seller where one party had control or significant influence over the other party. In other cases, the transaction may have been just one of several properties sold or traded between two parties. In such cases, the price paid for any particular piece is not it is market "value" (with the idea usually being, though, that all the bits and costs add up to the market value of all the parts) but rather it's market "price."

At other times, a buyer may willingly pay a premium price, above the generally accepted market value, if his subjective valuation of the property (its investment value for him) was higher than the market value. One specific example of this is an owner of a neighboring property who, by combining his wealth with the subject property, could obtain economies-of-scale. Similar situations sometimes happen in corporate finance. For example, this can occur when a merger or acquisition happens at a price which is higher than the value represented by the amount of the underlying stock. The usual explanation for these types of mergers and acquisitions is that "the sum is greater than its parts" since full ownership of a company provides full control of it. This is something that purchasers will sometimes pay a high price for. This situation can happen in real estate purchases too.

But the most common reason for value differing from price is that either the buyer or the seller is uninformed as to what a property's market value is but agrees on a contract at a specific price which is either too expensive or too cheap. This is unfortunate for one of the two parties. It is the obligation of a real property appraiser to estimate the actual market value of a property and not its market price .

SALES COMPARISON APPROACH

The sales comparison approach: The sales comparison approach is based primarily on the principle of substitution. This approach assumes a prudent (or rational) individual will pay no more for a property than it would cost to purchase a comparable substitute property. The approach recognizes that a typical buyer will compare asking prices and seek to buy the property that meets his or her wants and needs for the lowest cost. In developing the sales comparison approach, the appraiser attempts to interpret and measure the actions of parties involved in the marketplace, including buyers, sellers, and investors (comparing a property's characteristics with those of comparable properties that have recently sold in similar transactions).

Steps in the sales comparison approach

1. Research the market to obtain information about sales, and pending sales that are similar to the subject property

2. Investigate the market data to determine whether they are factually correct and accurate

3. Determine relevant units of comparison (e.g., sales price per square foot), and develop a comparative analysis for each

4. Compare the subject and comparable sales according to the elements of comparison and adjust as appropriate

5. Reconcile the multiple value indications that result from the adjustment (upward or downward) of the comparable sales into a single value indication

COST APPROACH

The cost approach: the buyer will not pay more for a property than it would cost to build one of three basic valuation methods. The others are the market approach, or a sales comparison approach, an income approach. The fundamental premise of the cost approach is that a potential user of real estate won't, or shouldn't, pay more for a property than it would cost to build an equivalent. The cost of construction minus depreciation, plus land, therefore is a limit, or at least a metric, of market value.

There are some reasonably large assumptions embedded here. One of the basics is that there is a sufficient supply of buildable land that construction is a viable alternative to purchase of an existing property. In some parts of the world today, including in the USA, there are areas which are either so fully developed or so restrictive in their planning approvals, that new construction is not an option because of the scarcity of land. A related question is whether the building in question is anything that would be built again in that market. If the trend of development favors, say, high volume warehousing, would anyone consider building a multi-story manufacturing facility? If the tendency is too high-density condominium buildings, would anyone consider building a detached house? The cost of constructing an obsolete building is regarded as not relevant to market value.

There are other methodological issues which can be problematic. How do you estimate the cost? Is it based on the reproduction of a replica or something that is judged to be functionally equivalent? Can you even estimate cost very precisely? When a project is put up to bid, is there not usually a range of prices offered for the same plans and specifications? Is the final cost of a project equal to the original bid? How should profit be treated? Some maintain that the cost approach will generally be the highest of the three methods. At the same time, it is a truism that a project is only feasible if its projected cost is less than its completed value.

In between new and obsolete various harmful elements related to age, fashion, and change (depreciation) will accrue. These are lumped into physical (wear, tear and deterioration), functional (look, feel, form and style), and vocational (the influence of factors outside the property itself).

It is generally considered that the cost approach gives the best indication of market value when the property in question is new and an appropriate (highest and best) use.

INCOME APPROACH

The Income Approach is one of three major groups of methodologies, called valuation approaches, used by appraisers. It is particularly common in commercial real estate appraisal and business appraisal. The fundamental math is similar to the methods used for financial valuation, securities analysis, or bond pricing. However, there are some significant and essential modifications when used in real estate or business valuation. While there are quite a few acceptable methods under the rubric of the income approach, most of these methods fall into three categories: direct capitalization, discounted cash flow, and gross income multiplier.

START TODAY

HOW TO START REAL ESTATE BUSINESS

PLANNING

He who fails to plan, plans to abandon. One has to have a business plan that's set one apart from the other real estate investors

to start real estate business one must plan properly. One must have a business plan to have a blueprint of what one wants to do. With an excellent real estate plan, one can set goals and have a focus. With planning, one can use it to get financial assistance from investors. It also helps to get involved directly in the real estate project. To plan also requires one to train one's brain how on how to think strategically about what is happening in the market and be ready to offer something of value to ones leads, no matter where they come from.

MARKET SURVEY

One must do market research to know how to relate. One must do the market early to save resources. One must find out if one has the right skill. One must also research to gain insight into real-world experience. One must also get a good mentor.

BRAND BUILDING

Branding helps to promote business. It helps to create a presentation to the market in the sight of the consumers. It helps the prospective client to know more OE have more perspective about one's business. Branding requires one to have a logo, an ad campaign, press release, etc. One must also build a good rapport with clients. One must stand out and created a distinct niche. One must be able to give client value for what they are paying.

FINANCE

Real estate business requires a tremendous amount of money. Hence one must have enough capital. If one is writing a business plan, one must approach the right investors and canvass them to one's side.

ONLINE PRESENCE

No matter how many locales one can indulge, there is still a need for the web presence to attract and engage online leads. Maintain the right online presence. One can also use social media presence as a marketing strategy.

CONCLUSION

So far, we have covered all of the critical strategies that you will need to begin your journey towards sustainable wealth by investing in real estate. It should be clear by now that by applying one or more of these strategies, you should be ready to retire early and create a lifetime of cash flow.

It is important to note, however, that even though real estate is a booming industry and has a lot of opportunities, you have to carry out your due diligence before making any decisions on how or when to invest. You should also make conscious efforts to improve your credit score while implementing these strategies so that you are better positioned to make the right call about your investments.

It is also essential that you build a strong network of people of like minds who will be able to help you with opportunities as they arise. Your system will also determine the kind of deals you can get as well as how timely you can be with your bids. Also, when you are faced with challenges and start thinking of quitting, the people you have around you will be the reason why you throw in the towel or why you keep on going.

Overall, your success in real estate investment depends more on you than any other person. The amount of work you are willing to put in per time will determine the kind of results you get. It is equally important that you continuously build upon your knowledge base and stay informed about rules and regulations that may impact your business. Also, you should learn how to stay ahead at all times.

Just like any other business, in real estate investment, learning never ends; so, never stop learning. And, after gathering the knowledge, ensure you apply it to your peculiar situation. There are no hard and fast rules when dealing with real estate, and you can easily carve out your path.

I am excited at the opportunities that lie ahead of you, and I look forward to reading your testimonies about the secrets you have learned from this book.

www.ingramcontent.com/pod-product-compliance
Lightning Source LLC
Chambersburg PA
CBHW071642210326
41597CB00017B/2086